Augmented Exploitation

Wildcat: Workers' Movements and Global Capitalism

Series Editors:
Immanuel Ness (City University of New York)
Peter Cole (Western Illinois University)
Raquel Varela (Instituto de História Contemporânea [IHC] of Universidade Nova de Lisboa, Lisbon New University)
Tim Pringle (SOAS, University of London)

Also available:

The Cost of Free Shipping: Amazon in the Global Economy
Edited by Jake Alimahomed-Wilson and Ellen Reese

Choke Points: Logistics Workers Disrupting the Global Supply Chain
Edited by Jake Alimahomed-Wilson and Immanuel Ness

Dying for an iPhone: Apple, Foxconn and the Lives of China's Workers
Jenny Chan, Mark Selden and Pun Ngai

Just Work? Migrant Workers' Struggles Today
Edited by Aziz Choudry and Mondli Hlatshwayo

Wobblies of the World: A Global History of the IWW
Edited by Peter Cole, David Struthers and Kenyon Zimmer

Organizing Insurgency: Workers' Movements in the Global South
Immanuel Ness

Southern Insurgency: The Coming of the Global Working Class
Immanuel Ness

Amakomiti: Grassroots Democracy in South African Shack Settlements
Trevor Ngwane

Workers' Inquiry and Global Class Struggle: Strategies, Tactics, Objectives
Edited by Robert Ovetz

The Spirit of Marikana: The Rise of Insurgent Trade Unionism in South Africa
Luke Sinwell with Siphiwe Mbatha

Solidarity: Latin America and the US Left in the Era of Human Rights
Steve Striffler

Working the Phones: Control and Resistance in Call Centres
Jamie Woodcock

Augmented Exploitation

Artificial Intelligence, Automation and Work

Edited by Phoebe V. Moore
and Jamie Woodcock

First published 2021 by Pluto Press
345 Archway Road, London N6 5AA

www.plutobooks.com

British Library Cataloguing in Publication Data
A catalogue record for this book is available from the British Library

ISBN 978 0 7453 4350 1 Hardback
ISBN 978 0 7453 4349 5 Paperback
ISBN 978 0 7453 4353 2 PDF eBook
ISBN 978 0 7453 4352 5 Kindle eBook
ISBN 978 0 7453 4351 8 EPUB eBook

This book is printed on paper suitable for recycling and made from fully managed and sustained forest sources. Logging, pulping and manufacturing processes are expected to conform to the environmental standards of the country of origin.

Typeset by Stanford DTP Services, Northampton, England

Simultaneously printed in the United Kingdom and United States of America

Contents

Figures

Series Preface

Workers' movements are a common and recurring feature in contemporary capitalism. The same militancy that inspired the mass labour movements of the twentieth century continues to define worker struggles that proliferate throughout the world today.

For more than a century, labour unions have mobilised to represent the political-economic interests of workers by uncovering the abuses of capitalism, establishing wage standards, improving oppressive working conditions, and bargaining with employers and the state. Since the 1970s, organised labour has declined in size and influence as the global power and influence of capital has expanded dramatically. The world over, existing unions are in a condition of fracture and turbulence in response to neoliberalism, financialisation, and the reappearance of rapacious forms of imperialism. New and modernised unions are adapting to conditions and creating a class-conscious workers' movement rooted in militancy and solidarity. Ironically, while the power of organised labour contracts, working-class militancy and resistance persists and is growing in the Global South.

Wildcat publishes ambitious and innovative works on the history and political economy of workers' movements and is a forum for debate on pivotal movements and labour struggles. The series applies a broad definition of the labour movement to include workers in and out of unions, and seeks works that examine proletarianisation and class formation; mass production; gender, affective and reproductive labour; imperialism and workers; syndicalism and independent unions, and labour and Leftist social and political movements.

Acknowledgements

Jamie Woodcock and Phoebe V. Moore would like to thank the organisers of the International Labour Process Conference (ILPC) 2019 in Vienna for accepting our stream on artificial intelligence and work. The contributors to this book presented in the stream, and we would like to acknowledge all of their efforts and contributions. A big thanks to David Shulman at Pluto for supporting the book idea, as well as to Robert Webb for guiding it through production. Each of the authors of the book were a pleasure to work with, particularly through the challenges of collecting final versions and changes through the Covid-19 pandemic.

When writing about work it is important to remember that there are already many people who keenly feel the effects of new technology in both recognised and unseen work. We therefore dedicate this book to all those workers finding new ways to make, fake, or break technology at work.

Phoebe V. Moore: I would like to acknowledge my mother Aureol for her steadfast support, and my father, Tom, for the same, over many years from PhD until now. My four brothers likewise, are continuously in my thoughts. I would also like to acknowledge Jamie Woodcock for being a very good co-organiser and co-editor.

Jamie Woodcock: I would like to thank my partner Lydia for her support throughout this project. I would also like to thank Phoebe V. Moore, both for coming up with the idea of an edited collection and for being a great collaborator and editor to work with.

Acknowledgements

Introduction
AI: Making it, Faking it, Breaking it

Phoebe V. Moore and Jamie Woodcock

Technology has shaped and reshaped work in various ways throughout history. Digital technology is continuing to create widespread change across different kinds of work, a process that is set to intensify with the increasing use of artificial intelligence (AI) and automation. So far, there has been documented use of AI in the hiring, managing and firing of workers. Less understood are the effects of this on the labour process, workers and managers more broadly. Although platform work uses AI extensively to plan, manage and control workers, there is limited empirical research on how these processes operate in practice.

There are two main problems with how AI and automation are discussed today. The first is a sense that they are somehow new and unprecedented interventions into the labour process. Historically, the machine is an attempt to automate *part* of the labour process, increasing the amount produced by a worker. It has a significantly longer history than self-driving cars or automated warehouse pickers. This leads us to the second problem: there is often a binary understanding of automation, either something will be automated or not. This leads to a focus on the machine – how effective is the new self-driving vehicle, for example – rather than looking at how automation is actually affecting work and workers. Rather than an either/or, automation is used much more as an *augmentation* of the labour process. While the word 'augmentation' is often used to refer to improvement, the editors of this volume intend to challenge not only this definitional substance but the concept altogether. While automation and machinic augmentation can work to improve workers' lives, in the context of neoliberal capitalism there is a broad assumption that technology will streamline work and make organisations more efficient, rather than an interrogation of the dangers and risks that accompany the processes outlined in the following chapters.

To address these challenges the contributions to this volume address the issues of AI, automation and work through three lines of analysis. First, we look at how AI is 'made', exploring how AI comes into being and how it is used, e.g., in human resource decision-making; how workers are becoming resources for machines in the sense of training AI datasets as 'AI trainers'; how we are being oriented in the workplace as though we are either working in direct competition with machines or working for them as our managers; and focusing as well on the work of software developers. Second, the line of analysis of 'faking', referring to the increased use of AI as a smokescreen to hide managerial decision-making processes and accountability. And third, authors look at 'breaking' the system that surrounds AI and automation practices, highlighting worker resistance, both emergent and potential.

In digitalised work studies, empirical and theoretical research on platform and gig work (see editors' work in this area Woodcock and Graham 2019; Moore and Joyce 2019 and further extensive references in this collection), have made important headway in the literature and made an impact on government policy such as the UK's Taylor report (Taylor 2017). Now, adding to these critical interventions, algorithmic governance and AI-augmented tools are increasingly also being used to make decisions about workers and in other forms of work beyond delivery and ride sharing. Disentangling the ways in which AI works in practice, as well as understanding how it can be resisted, are increasingly pressing concerns for both workers and researchers. This volume's three-part understanding of AI provides the basis for a much-needed debate on these rapidly emerging issues. The problem is not that we are not socially evolving to keep up with technologies, as Zuboff speculated (2015: 82). It is rather that powerful users of technologies running aggressive multinational and national companies, governments and other public and private actors, are racing to the top by investing heavily in research and development in the uses of AI for profiling workers, while simultaneously racing to the bottom by finding the newest and most innovative ways to keep wages and worker representation as minimal as possible.

PART I: MAKING IT

The first part of this book focuses on 'making it'. Here, we collect five chapters on the processes, decisions and dynamics involved in the work of making artificial intelligence and its application in the workplace. In the first chapter, Phoebe V. Moore asks 'Who is the Smart Worker Today?', drawing on her previous work on the quantified self. She develops this into an understanding of what kind of intelligence is expected from machines and how this then impacts the kinds of intelligences expected from the new smart worker. The implications are considered for what kinds of outcomes these new smart workers will face, how they can resist, and the wider complications that this will create for automation and workplace surveillance.

In Chapter 2, 'Work Now, Profit Later: AI Between Capital, Labour and Regulation', Toni Prug and Paško Bilić focus on the actors that promote and invest in AI futures, as well as considering the large investments – both of capital and labour – required to try and make these futures a reality. Taking a Marxist approach to analysing these dynamics, they begin by focusing on the concentration and centralisation of capital that has driven investment in AI. In particular, they note that while AI promises to be a general form of technology with wide applications, the promised outcomes have not yet materialised. The chapter then moves on to discuss the ways in which capital relies on both highly skilled and high-paid labour in software development, and an increasingly hidden and globally dispersed workforce required to train machine learning algorithms. The lack of effective regulation is then considered, in relation to the development of AI understood in the context of the contradictions of capitalist production. The strength of this analysis lies in its tracing of the relationships of power and exploitation through the financing and production of AI, demonstrating that the current future of AI is one dominated by capital, but that this need not be the case.

In Chapter 3, 'Delivering Food on Bikes: Between Machinic Subordination and Autonomy in the Algorithmic Workplace', Benjamin Herr takes a Marxist Labour Process Theory approach to understanding the algorithms used in food-delivery platforms. Drawing on empirical evidence, the chapter focuses on the experience of people being managed by algorithms. As Herr reminds us, 'algorithms are consciously constructed and implemented in the capitalist labour process to discipline and control labour'. The centring of food-delivery workers' experience provides a much needed focus on the problems of the technology in practice. Herr builds on the argument of the 'illusion of freedom' (Waters and Woodcock 2017), analysing the operation of the algorithm and workers' experience of it. This understanding of how the algorithm is made to work in practice is crucial for a critical analysis of this kind of work. After all, as Herr notes, organising starts with workers and 'how [they] perceive their work and the technology applied'. The chapter foreshadows some of the volume's later discussions of resistance, providing an important backdrop for what follows.

Eduard Müller's chapter, 'Putting the Habitus to Work: Digital Prosumption, Surveillance and Distinction', focuses on the overlaps between production and consumption, using this as a starting point for understanding the implications of digital technology. It starts with a return to the debates on the 'prosumer', considering how these can be expanded in data-driven surveillance contexts. In particular, the chapter reintroduces Bourdieu's notion of 'habitus', updating it in the light of surveillance capitalism and applying it to an organisational context. Müller therefore draws attention to the blurring of boundaries between work and leisure, accelerated through platform technology. While questions of power are often brought to the fore in research on digitalisation, particularly via Foucault, this chapter argues that future research can benefit from drawing on Bourdieu, unpicking the role of the customers' habitus which plays an increasingly important role in relation to organisations. This commodification of the habitus represents an important area for future research, further developing critical understandings of the shifting relationships of digitalisation.

In Chapter 5, Uwe Vormbusch and Peter Kels discuss 'The Power of Prediction: People Analytics at Work'. The topic of data is considered again, this time focusing on the application of new forms of people analytics in the workplace. This is situated within longer histories of control, both at work and more widely, that represent attempts to control the future, introducing new forms of governmentality. The chapter begins by critically examining people analytics, drawing attention to its use of automation and algorithms in the screening, analysis and processing of data. The authors consider how potential applications could be found across human resource management, seeking to transform decision-making at work, before moving on to analyse how Predictive People Analytics practices are currently being implemented. This draws attention to the way in which automated decision-making is made opaque to the user – both workers and managers – undermining their ability to either understand or contest the choices made. The discussion focuses on the limitations of these practices, in particular on how they involve social normalisation and coercion, failing to take into account the diversity of ways in which people work. The authors conclude that these practices could lead to resistance – or serious legal challenges – as they concentrate economic power in the hands of new data-science specialists.

PART II: FAKING IT

The second part of the book moves on to discuss 'faking it', highlighting the limits of algorithms and automation. In particular, there have been examples in which capital pretends to be using artificial intelligence – often to gain attention or the kudos of being engaged in this kind of high technology work. In reality, behind the scenes, there is a worker. This section is therefore a brief walk to the end of the yellow brick road of artificial intelligence, pulling back the curtain on contemporary claims. In Chapter 6, Luca Perrig discusses 'Manufacturing Consent in the Gig Economy'. His chapter draws on empirical research with local platforms in Switzerland. Perrig worked for each of the five major platforms over the course of six months. He interviewed couriers and managers, and conducted a month-long ethnography with platform managers in their offices. This detailed empirical data is used to re-pose the question asked by Burawoy (1979) and others: why do workers work as hard as they do? Taking a starting point that is critical of the platform model, the chapter identifies the challenges this model faces in practice. Given the widespread use of self-employment status, Perrig discusses the problems that this precarious arrangement creates for consent at work, further complicated by the reliance on online communication. Starting from these challenges is a refreshing approach. Rather than starting from the victory of capital, Perrig interrogates how the platform model operates. In particular, he focuses on the attempted automation of the management function, using a combination of differential delivery fees, techniques of gamification, and the control of information. Each of these are used to try and maximise the number of transactions that workers agree to. Rather than concluding that an algorithm has solved these issues, Perrig's chapter instead inquires into the role of platforms as market intermediaries, examining how they shape the markets behind the use of automation.

In Chapter 7, 'Automated and Autonomous? Technologies Mediating the Exertion and Perception of Labour Control', Beatriz Casas González re-examines the long-running debate in Labour Process Theory between technological change and labour autonomy. She focuses on two empirical case studies of German manufacturing companies, one in electronics and the other in communication technologies. The chapter addresses issues from the author's PhD project on technologically mediated influence over workers' perception of control. It finds that there are two main impacts: on the one hand, new technologies are used as part of a broader strategy to directly control labour in the factory, reducing workers' decision-making opportunities and actions. On the other hand, technologies are also introduced as part of a strategy of control that relies on worker agency. These different dynamics are found within the same workplace, creating contradictions and strains which workers are left to resolve. However, workers do not identify either of these dynamics with greater control over their work. This raises important questions about the understanding of technology as neutral. The chapter concludes by emphasising the importance of workers' perceptions of how these technologies operate in practice, considering how this either reproduces the control of capital or could lead to its disruption.

In Chapter 8, Giorgio Boccardo asks 'Can Robots Produce Customer Confidence?', drawing on an extensive case study of the Chilean banking sector, including 13 years of labour market data, 36 interviews, and an eight-year ethnography. This focuses on examining the labour process – which shares common characteristics with the sector in other countries. The question of automation is explored first through the longer trends of technological change within the banking sector, and then automation is considered in practice through the specificities of the banking labour process. In particular, Boccardo discusses the boundaries and limits to automation in relation to how confidence is produced and reproduced between banks and their clients. This problematises automation, unpacking its complexities in practice. The chapter concludes by arguing that automation needs to be placed within the existing relations of power, and asks whether trade unions can transform these relations to produce positive outcomes for automation.

PART III: BREAKING IT

The third part of the book discusses 'breaking it'. Here, the focus shifts towards the new ways that workers are finding to resist the use of algorithms and automation at work. We frame this last part as 'breaking' in order to draw attention to the long and complex history of resistance to – and with – technology. Going beyond the usual trope of machine breaking, the chapters examine how workers resist the new relations of production. This can involve directly resisting technology, but attention is drawn to the wider resistance to management in the labour process. The chapters in this final part build on arguments in the first two parts, in terms of both how these technologies are made and the gaps that emerge from aspects of 'fakeness' in their practical application. The volume thus shifts onto the terrain of struggle, considering both how workers can resist and are resisting, as well as how they can reshape their own conditions in this new context.

The first chapter in this section, Adam Badger's 'It Gets Better With Age: AI and the Labour Process in Old and New Gig-Economy Firms', focuses on platform delivery work. It first situates this kind of work within the longer history of couriers, examining how different technology has been applied to manage the delivery labour process. The platformisation of this work is rooted in both the development of AI technologies as well as the interests of shareholder investments. Platforms are understood here through Srnicek's (2017) analysis of platform capitalism, critically analysed through Badger's extensive ethnographic engagement with the work in London. Through a comparison of two rival platforms, the chapter highlights the importance of data generation to the business model. Badger's fieldwork identifies how workers respond to the contradictions of the labour process, often 'multi-apping' in order to maximise their pay. He draws attention not only to the highly visible resistance of strikes and protests, but also to the micro practices through which workers contest the algorithm in their daily work.

In Chapter 10, 'Self-Tracking and Sousveillance at Work', Marta E. Cecchinato, Sandy Gould and Frederick Harry Pitts combine Labour Process Theory with insights from Human-Computer Interaction (HCI). While many critical accounts of surveillance and self-tracking have focused on the capacity of these techniques to strengthen management in the labour process, this chapter asks whether there are new collective potentials in the forms of data collection, aggregation and curation. This account of 'breaking it' is therefore one of breaking with the original purpose of the technology, and instead considering alternative and possibly emancipatory uses. The authors discuss the different managerial uses of these techniques, as well as the self-tracking individualised uses. The concept of 'sousveillance' is introduced as an inversion of the surveillance, in order to consider the possibilities for bottom-up practices of surveillance, taking the side of workers instead of management.

In Chapter 11, 'Breaking Digital Atomisation: Resistant Cultures of Solidarity in Platform-Based Courier Work', Heiner Heiland and Simon Schaupp discuss the labour process of food platform delivery work. The authors engaged in autoethnographic fieldwork as food couriers for Deliveroo and Foodora in six different cities; conducted 47 interviews with food couriers across seven different German cities; carried out a survey; and undertook a content analysis of forums and chat groups. From this data, they argue that while platforms attempt full control over the labour process and the atomising of workers, the reality from the workers' perspective tells a different story. They explore how riders stay in regular contact, both on the streets but also through online communication methods, and argue that these forms of communication are the building blocks for practices of solidarity and collective action. Resisting atomisation, workers have found ways to self-organise within the labour process. Heiland and Schaupp note that communication alone is not sufficient for developing collective solidarity. They trace how this has emerged in practice, focusing first on self-organisation and the role of radical trade unions, as well as the later involvement of more traditional trade unions. Throughout, the chapter critiques the argument that artificial intelligence at work has been able to solve the problems of control for capital in the labour process.

In the final chapter of this collection, Joanna Bronowicka and Mirela Ivanova's 'Resisting the Algorithmic Boss: Guessing, Gaming, Reframing and Contesting Rules in App-based Management', the authors' aim is to understand the relationship between algorithmic management and resistance practices on food-delivery platforms. Drawing on extensive fieldwork in Berlin with Foodora and Deliveroo riders, the chapter discusses practices through which workers attempt to 'break' the algorithm. Bronowicka and Ivanova argue that algorithmic management introduces three additional pressures in the labour process of delivery workers: the withholding of information; a lack of feedback mechanisms to workers; and methods of performance control that rely on data. From these tensions in the labour process, the workers in this case study have developed a repertoire of resistance practices. First, they engage in processes of 'guessing the algorithm', attempting to understand the choices being made. These become collective processes that workers engage in together. Second, they find ways to game the system, seeking out ways to bypass the rules of the algorithm. Third, they reframe the work, particularly developing collective grievances in their meeting points away from the management's (or the algorithm's) gaze. Finally, workers also directly contest the algorithmic decision-making process with collective protests and strikes.

REFERENCES

Burawoy, M. (1979). *Manufacturing Consent*. Chicago: University of Chicago Press.

Moore, P. and Joyce, S. (2020). Black Box or Hidden Abode? The Expansion and Exposure of Platform Work Managerialism. Special Issue 'The Political Economy of Management', ed. Samuel Knafo and Matthew Eagleton-Pierce. *Review of International Political Economy* 27(3).

Srnicek, N. (2017). *Platform Capitalism*. Cambridge: Polity.

Taylor, M. (2017) Good Work: The Taylor Review of Modern Working Practices. At www.gov.uk/government/publications/good-work-the-taylor-review-of-modern-working-practices.

Waters, F. and Woodcock, J. (2017). Far from Seamless: A Workers' Inquiry at Deliveroo. *Viewpoint Magazine*. At www.viewpointmag.com/2017/09/20/far-seamless-workers-inquiry-deliveroo.

Woodcock, J. and Graham, M. (2019). *The Gig Economy: A Critical Introduction*. Cambridge: Polity.

Zuboff, S. (2015). Big Other: Surveillance Capitalism and the Prospects of an Information Civilization. *Journal of Information Technology* 30, 75–89.

PART I

Making It

1
AI Trainers: Who is the Smart Worker Today?

Phoebe V. Moore

Most scholarly and governmental discussions about artificial intelligence (AI) today focus on a country's technological competitiveness and try to identify how this supposedly new technological capability will improve productivity. Some discussions look at AI ethics. But AI is more than a technological advancement. It is a social question and requires philosophical inquiry. From the time of the Victorians who built tiny machines resembling maids, to the development of humanoid carebots such as are seen in Japan today, we have been reifying machines with our characteristics. Malabou (2015) discusses the cyberneticians' assumptions that intelligence is primarily associated with reason as per the Enlightenment ethos. Indeed, cyberneticists' fascination with similarities between living tissue and nerves and electronic circuitry 'gave rise to darker man-machine fantasies: zombies, living dolls, robots, brain washing, and hypnotism' (Pinto 2015: 31). Pasquinelli (2015) argues that cybernetics, AI and current 'algorithmic capitalism' researchers believed and still believe in instrumental or technological rationality and the ontological and epistemological determinism and positivism that permeate these assumptions. The mysticism and curiosity about how smart machines can be, and how this is manifest, predates our current era. But unlike in the first stages of AI research, where scholars such as Hubert Dreyfus (1979) directly challenged the idea that it would be relatively easy to get a machine to behave as though it were a human, today very little AI research looks for a relationship between the machine and the workings of the human mind. Nonetheless, software engineers and designers – and software users, who in the cases set out below are human resource professionals and managers – unconsciously as well as consciously project direct forms of intelligence onto machines themselves, without considering in any depth the practical nor philosophical implications of this, when weighed against human actual or perceived intelligences. Neither do they think about the relations of production that are required for the development and production of AI and its capabilities, where workers are expected not only to accept the intelligences of machines, now called 'smart machines', but also to endure particularly difficult working conditions in the process of creating and expanding the datasets that are required for the development of AI itself.

If AI does actually become as prevalent and as significant as predictions would have it – and we really do make ourselves the direct mirror reflection of machines, and/or simply resources for fuelling them through the production of datasets via our own supposed intelligence of, e.g., image recognition – then we will have a very real set of problems on our hands. Potentially, workers will only be necessary for machinic maintenance or, as discussed later in this chapter, as AI trainers. AI is often linked to automation and potential job losses, but very little discussion of the quality of jobs that replace previously existing jobs is occurring. AI is not automation, in fact. AI is most suitably described as an augmentation tool and/or application that builds on data collection and allows advances in dataset usage and decision-making, rather than as a stand-alone entity. While the Internet of Things, automation and digitalisation sometimes overlap with discussions of AI, the European Commission's more precise definition of AI in its 2020 White Paper is quite useful: a 'collection of technologies that combine data, algorithms and computing power. Advances in computing and the increasing availability of data are therefore key drivers of the current upsurge of AI' (European Commission 2020). The European Commission's definition as provided in its 2018 Communication is also useful in indicating that AI 'refers to systems that display intelligent behaviour by analysing their environment and taking actions – with some degree of autonomy – to achieve specific goals' (European Commission 2018). A 2018 report for the European Parliament's Committee on Industry, Research and Energy, entitled 'European Artificial Intelligence Leadership, the Path for an Integrated Vision', defines AI as a 'cover term for techniques associated with data analysis and pattern recognition' (Delponte 2018: 11).

In 2019, the OECD published its 'Recommendations of the Council on Artificial Intelligence', stating that AI will be a good opportunity for 'augmenting human capabilities and enhancing creativity, advancing inclusion of underrepresented populations, reducing economic, social, gender and other inequalities, and protecting natural environments, thus invigorating inclusive growth, sustainable development and well-being' (OECD 2019), and differentiating AI from other digital technologies in that 'AI are set to learn from their environments in order to take autonomous decisions'.

These definitions not only identify the scope and context within which AI is understood to have the potential to affect workspaces, but also take into account the often incorrect blanket use of the term. AI machines and systems are seen to demonstrate competences which are increasingly similar to human decision-making and prediction. AI-augmented tools and applications are intended to improve human resources and allow more sophisticated tracking of productivity, attendance and even health data for workers. These tools are often seen to perform much faster and more accurately than humans and, thus, managers.

However, as Aloisi and Gramano (2019) point out, once management is fully automated, AI may also engender or push forward 'authoritative attitudes ... perpetuate bias, promote discrimination, and exacerbate inequality, thus paving the way to social unrest and political turmoil'. Sewell (2005) warned of the ways in which nudges and penalties introduced by AI-augmented incentivisation schemes can create tensions within working situations, and Tucker (2019) cautioned that AI-influenced ranking systems and metrics can be 'manipulated and repurposed to infer unspecified characteristics or to predict unknown behaviours' (discussed in Aloisi and Gramano 2019: 119).

This chapter paves the way for discussions in later chapters of *Augmented Exploitation*, through exploring the ontological premise for recognising human 'intelligence' in machines. Exploitation in the labour process relation is tried and tested and widely reported. Workers resist, often also in highly creative ways. However, the forms of control discussed in work and organisation studies are no longer restricted to the analogue but are now increasingly augmented through sophisticated or 'smart' technological capabilities. Neither Marx nor subsequent Marxist, Marxian or post-Marxist researchers fully acknowledged or interrogated the assumptions around what is necessary scientifically to build an intelligent machine, or what we today call a smart machine, given that defining the 'smart' or 'intelligent' human is already highly problematic in itself.

After outlining smart machines' demonstrations of seeming and hoped-for intelligences, and then indicating how that is translated into explicit social relations of production, this chapter makes the argument that workers, in collaboration, should be appropriating and intervening in the understandings of 'smart', to critique and challenge the dominant ideas surrounding supposed machinic smartness or intelligence. A range of human resources assistive machines seen in 'people analytics' have, after all, shown evidence of discriminatory, racist, sexist and psychosocially violent traits of human intelligence in digitalised work contexts. If these are the core tenets of the dominant forms of human intelligence today, then we may or perhaps should be heading for a new phase of lines of questioning, where these assumptions must be challenged. In that light, this chapter begins a discussion to devise a means for a war of position, in the Gramscian sense, for the smart worker today.

SMART MACHINES

We hear about smart cars, smartphones, smart watches and even smart cities in the news and in scientific research, but there seems to be no critique around what 'smart' means. Heuristically, we can say that 'smart' as a definitional category for these kinds of objects refers to machines' ability to perform an activity on behalf of humans, or to perfect reality for us by performing menial tasks, providing convenience and services, and enhancing possibilities for ecological sustainability. Smart cars are smaller than average and can run on electricity instead of petrol, thereby helping the environment and so hopefully extending humans' stay on this planet. Smart cars are also expected to eliminate the need for a human driver altogether. Low productivity in the UK has been attributed to the time wasted in commuting to work. If we are being driven to work by robots, we could read our Kindles and write on our iPads in the back seat, relying on the intelligence of machines and at the same time ideally developing our own. We might even eliminate 'bullshit jobs' (Graeber 2018) through achieving more quality work, upskilling and so on, and improving the country's productivity altogether.

Of course, these utopian ideas could be stymied due to the Covid-19 global pandemic, as a result of which many knowledge workers are increasingly being required to stay home to work. The 'smart office' may thus increasingly come to be defined within the laboratory of personal environments, where a range of devices used to calculate working time electronically and to measure other aspects of work are normalised via experimentation. Smartphones offer a further chance for work mobility in terms of documenting workers' geographical position and offering the use of the internet and a camera. Phone conversations in which we can see people's faces, as well as the array of applications enabling us to find our way to the nearest restaurant or shop, listen to almost any music we want, track patterns in our steps and heart rate, order transport, set goals, do yoga, read books and get the latest news, are other features of smartphones that can be used for workplace benefit. 'Smart cities', furthermore, provide convenience for citizens and tourists in terms of better connectedness and travel options.

While these smart products and environments sound quite attractive and exciting, they rely on the acquisition of big datasets extracted from human activity or objects that are based originally in human activity. Self-driving cars must learn to recognise specific images which are originally categorised by human labour. Smartphones' provisions such as digital maps rely on data about locations provided by human input. The smart office relies on data collected from workers' keystrokes, timestamps for entering and exiting work platforms, and so on. With regards to smart services and social media, products are provided in exchange for, in some cases, a small monetary fee, or, more often than not, in the expectation that the reams of data gathered about us will be used to profile our 'selves' for advertising and possibly for governmental use.

Based on human data, smart technologies, via machine learning, algorithms, robotics and emotion coding, demonstrate a series of forms of active 'smarts' or intelligences which I have previously categorised as collaborative, assistive, prescriptive and proscriptive (Moore 2020), where machines' functionality towards these active intelligences is facilitated and augmented by AI. These are human/machine mirror intelligences, but they are based more on *active potential* than on expected *social cognitive conditions* which then are evidenced in what Marx referred to as the social relations of production. This chapter therefore builds on my previous arguments about human/machine reflections of intelligence, looking more closely at the social relations of production and the surrounding expectations placed on the smart worker.

AI TRAINERS AND THE RELATIONS OF PRODUCTION

Karl Marx observed, in the 'Fragment on Machines' section of *Grundrisse: Foundations of the Critique of Political Economy* (Marx 1993), that we as humans often attribute to machines our own characteristics, and, by association, also intelligence. However, since the site of introduction into the labour process is one of class struggle, the attribution of intelligence to machines relies on specific categories of 'intelligence' in socially dominant understandings of that sphere. As Marx observed, the employment relationship in the early stages of industrialisation divided people along class lines, whereby a handful of people were assumed to have the superior intelligence required to design machines and to organise and manage workplaces, as well as manage workers and control labour processes and operations. The other main category for intelligence explicitly subordinated workers, who were expected to carry out physical labour and to build and maintain the very same machines that were ultimately considered to be more intelligent than the average person.

All this being said, intelligence is by no means a homogeneous category, and so-called symbolic and connectionist AI researchers have never got to grips with nor agreed on what the most important features of intelligence are. John Haugeland, who coined the term 'GOFAI', described intelligent beings as demonstrating the following characteristics:

> our ability to deal with things intelligently ... due to our capacity to think about them reasonably (including subconscious thinking); and the capacity to think about things reasonably [which] amounts to a faculty for internal 'automatic' symbol manipulation. (Haugeland 1985: 113)

Marcus Hutter, who designed a well-known theory of universal AI, later argued: 'The human mind ... is connected to consciousness and identity which define who we are ... Intelligence is the most distinct characteristic of the human mind ... It enables us to understand, explore, and considerably shape our world, including ourselves.' AI research, Hutter indicates, reflects this sentiment, since the 'grand goal of AI is to develop systems that exhibit general intelligence on a human-level or beyond' (Hutter 2012: 1). Empathy and sentience; memory and the distinctly human ability to process thoughts and ideas and turn those ideas into analysis; the ability to make choices rather than simple decisions – all these are necessary for intelligence to be manifest, which is particularly important as machines are ascribed more forms of intelligence. In these ways, the machine may soon come to be understood as autonomous.

AUTONOMOUS SMARTS

The most important prediction and hope in 1956, which is still widely appreciated today, is that machines will *learn* and even *teach themselves*, and that this is what defines them as being intelligent, or what we now refer to as smart. While there have been various phases in expectations of their capability, to finalise the goal towards universal AI, the goal in the current phase of research and development is for machines to be fully autonomous.

'Universal', autonomous AI is where a single universal agent can learn to behave optimally in any environment, where universal competences are demonstrated by a robot, such as walking, seeing and talking, and where machines can teach themselves by using errors to adapt and optimise algorithms in order to 'perform' better the next time. Today, as computer memory capacity increases, and programmes become more sophisticated, universal AI is becoming an increasingly likely prospect. This would lead to a machine that can learn, teach itself, and even teach people and, of course, workers.

Despite the current expectation for machines to be autonomous, however, direct comparisons with human thought, being and competences in AI research have all but disappeared. This is a problem, because AI is bursting back into public discourse, while generating a huge resurgence in corporate interest and attracting major investments of government funding (even as local austerity initiatives and the funding of unpopular wars continue). The European Commission's definition of AI quoted earlier in this chapter emphasises the autonomous aspects of the kind of intelligence expected of machines: specifically, AI 'refers to systems that display intelligent behaviour by analysing their environment and taking actions – with some degree of *autonomy* – to achieve specific goals' (European Commission 2018; emphasis added). This definition should facilitate a clear discussion about what is at stake as AI systems and machines are integrated into workplaces, making decisions and predictions much faster and more accurately than humans can, while exhibiting human-like behaviour and assisting workers, with, so it is hoped, full autonomy. Indeed, workers are now expected not only, for all intents and purposes, to be controlled and managed by machines portrayed as universally reliable calculators, but also to potentially mimic and learn from them, rather than the other way round.

The idea of autonomy is thus central to all discussions about AI today, but the agency ascribed to the human by definition is not identical to the concept applied to machines. A series of social movements and activist groups have taken autonomy exceedingly seriously since the 1960s, such as the Italian *autonomia* movement, which took issue with the dominance of the Catholic Church and with the power of the bourgeoisie to impose work and working conditions that eliminated the human capacity for expression and solidarity. Here, human autonomy is linked explicitly to activism and social justice. The autonomous robot is rarely described as agential in the same regard. New materialism and post-humanist research have gone some way in exploring conatus and material objects and our relations to them, but to align the way human autonomy is, and historically has been, comprehended with how AI autonomy is understood today would be absurd.

Instead, autonomous machines, rather than pose a challenge to the status quo in the workplace, are expected to willingly include and work with another actor with apparent agency and autonomy to the standard employment relationship. This actor is, of course, a supposedly autonomous machine. Its autonomy is understood to be demonstrated via its capabilities for analysis and prediction in 'people analytics'; via automation and semi-automation which is part of its supposed 'assistive' and 'collaborative' intelligence; and all of this via the machine's extensive surveillance capabilities.

WHO TRAINS THE AI?

Having looked at the types of intelligence attributed to machines both consciously and subconsciously by the engineers and software developers designing and building them and their applications, we now turn to a discussion of the backbone of AI and its development. This relies upon the production of big datasets that require human labour, at least in their early stages. In this context, swathes of semi- and un-skilled workers in both the Global North and South are carrying out digital 'dirty work' (Roberts 2016) in social media and data services. This category of what we can call 'AI trainers' includes a) content moderators, who curate content for social media platforms such as Facebook and other news and video services, and b) data service workers, who work with data via annotation and natural language process training for such products as Amazon's chatbot Alexa. These 'information service workers' (Gray 2019) usually work in opaque conditions

(Anwar and Graham 2019). The main, and very lucrative, asset they provide is the information needed for huge databases of images and text which are used to train machines for AI, thereby adding significant value to social media and smart devices, while also contributing to the development of AI. AI trainers have been referred to as 'ghost workers' (Gray and Suri 2019) and 'internet custodians' (Gillespie 2018), and as workers who are themselves expected to behave like machines (Ruckenstein and Turenen 2019).

While there are trade secrets around what precisely happens to the datasets these workers create, discussions I have had with several technical experts reveal that companies use the datasets generated by AI training (AIT) work to train other products. For example, Facebook uses deep learning networks to train machines to recognise human emotions from images (Facebook 2020). Google offers an 'Explicit Content Detection' product that can correctly identify five different categories of content (Google 2019). While Microsoft offers its Azure Content Moderator for the detection, moderation and filtering of various images, text and videos (Microsoft 2020). Some of these products could eventually automate AIT work itself, however, human AIT roles remain the norm in today's digital workforce and they are not likely to be fully automated any time soon, if at all. Currently, the tasks AI trainers carry out require human involvement and cognitive work that it is not yet possible to fully automate (Gillespie 2018). In fact, all algorithmic enforcement and decision-making systems are difficult, if not impossible, to automate (Perel and Elkin-Koren 2017), due to the sensitive, subjective nature of the work as well as liability issues surrounding decision-making.

Companies do not publicly release data on how many workers are currently carrying out content moderation or natural language process training specifically, but there were 6.1 million data workers in Europe in 2016 (IDC and Open Evidence 2017), and at least 41,000 content moderators globally (Levin 2017; Newton 2019). The World Bank projected that the online outsourcing industry would grow from USD4.8 billion in 2016 to up to 25 billion in 2020 (World Bank 2015). Given these trends and the enormous ongoing investment in AI, this workforce is highly representative of the future of work (Gray 2019). In both hemispheres, and similar to gig workers, AI trainers represent an unskilled or semi-skilled, low paid and insecure category of digital workers who are most at risk in times of crisis and change. Research about, and the exposure of, gig work is now impacting policy across the world, but AIT workers have no correspondent coverage. Like gig workers, AI trainers are 'on-demand', carrying out non-standard, task-based jobs, for which they are offered limited contracts with very little in the way of social protections such as union membership rights. Digital workers in lower skilled tiers face very high levels of exposure to psychosocial violence (Moore 2018a, 2020; D'Cruz and Noronha 2018), experience exceedingly unsafe workplaces (Newton 2019), and are subject to extreme levels of monitoring and surveillance (Noronha and D'Cruz 2009). Indeed, one group of content moderators is currently suing Facebook due to work-related post-traumatic stress disorder (Wong 2020).

On top of these augmented exploitations, AI trainers perform an element of unpaid and unseen work that adds significant value to the development of AI products. The paid work of AI trainers is recognised and their productivity measured through intensive ticketing systems, time tracking and digitised performance monitoring. In contrast, significant invisiblised and unpaid work is not ticketed or tracked in the same way, but is carried out through 'affective labour'. Affective labour is the mostly unseen surplus work performed by AI trainers to protect themselves from the trauma caused by, for example, the horrifying images content moderators report seeing many times daily, as well as the stress of being heavily digitally monitored, and the internal mechanisms they must unconsciously adopt in order to cope with the work (Levin 2017; Newton 2019; Punsmann 2018). AI trainer content moderators experience trauma on behalf of consumers of social media.

THE SMART WORKER'S DATA RIGHTS

So far, I have discussed the types of intelligences ascribed to machines and the relations of production that are required for the datasets upon which those perceived intelligences are built. Indeed, AI cannot exist without human data. Thus, in this section, I look at the rights a 'smart worker' has, or should have, to protect their working conditions – whether as a data trainer, gig worker, or any other digitalised worker – when it comes to the protection of the data that is gathered about them while they simultaneously produce data themselves.

The EU's General Data Protection Regulation (GDPR) will be the focus for this set of arguments, because, as a policy instrument, it introduces extensive updates to older versions of data and privacy policy, and a new set of possibilities for workers' rights in relation to institutional data collection, processing and usage. While many assume this Regulation is mostly applicable to consumers, it also contains extensive worker protections. Introduced to replace the 1995 Data Protection Directive (DPD), the GDPR allows for better discussions between workers and management about the seeming necessity for data collection; establishes proportionality between a company's stated necessity to collect data and workers' data protection and privacy rights and other needs; requires transparency when data collection and other tracking and monitoring processes are considered; emphasises the importance of data minimisation, where companies should only collect as much data as is needed to achieve an intended goal; and covers many other areas that concern digital workers.

The GDPR is a game-changer in terms of providing ammunition for trade union representatives in collective bargaining, and particularly, for example, in the important area of 'consent'. The concept of consent was defined in the 1995 DPD (EU 95/46/EC) as 'any freely given specific and informed indication of his [*sic*] wishes by which the data subject signifies his agreement to personal data relating to him being processed'. The GDPR definition goes further, so that the way consent is sought, and given, is now also under scrutiny. The GDPR's Art. 4(11) makes it clear that consent is 'any freely given, specific, informed and unambiguous indication of the data subject's wishes by which he or she, by a statement or by a clear affirmative action, signifies agreement to the processing of personal data relating to him or her'. Art. 7 and recitals 32, 33, 42 and 43 provide guidance on the ways the Data Controller (usually the organisation or institution which employs workers and collects data about them) must behave in order to meet the main elements of the consent requirement. Recital 32 provides a particularly good clarification:

> Consent should be given by a clear affirmative act establishing a freely given, specific, informed and unambiguous indication of the data subject's agreement to the processing of personal data relating to him or her, such as by a written statement, including by electronic means, or an oral statement.

'Freely given' consent, of course, is only possible in a situation where a data subject has a say and a real choice. As the 2020 update published by the European Data Protection Board (EDPB) indicates: 'if the data subject has no real choice, feels compelled to consent or will endure negative consequences if they do not consent, then consent will not be valid'. Furthermore, if it is 'bundled up' and 'non-negotiable', or a subject cannot refuse or withdraw consent without detriment, then consent has not been freely offered (EDPB 2020: 7). While these explicit interventions are promising in relation to consumers – where for years now, data accumulation has substituted for more traditional forms of payment for services – consent is difficult to authentically obtain in the employment relationship due to its inherently imbalanced nature.

However, given the discussion around whether workers can meaningfully give consent for data collection and use, meaningful *dissent* to the possible violations of privacy and data protections that workers face is also increasingly possible. GDPR Recital 32 lists some important aspects of the new requirements, indicating radical new regulations, such as the stipulation that 'silence, pre-ticked boxes or inactivity should not ... constitute consent'.

The EDPB 2020 Guidelines therefore recommend that 'requirements for consent under the GDPR are not considered to be an "additional obligation", but rather as preconditions for lawful processing' (EDPB 2020: 6). While consent is only one of six criteria that may be selected by a company to identify the lawfulness of its actions, consent to data collection and processing is nevertheless worth keeping alive in discussions, particularly if co-determination is legislated, and during collective bargaining between employers and worker representative groups. Consent could take a different form, intellectually overhauled and reconsidered in definitional terms when discussing unions to be meaningful *if obtained via unions* rather than simply individually.

For quite obvious reasons, the concept of consent does not necessarily sit easily with worker/manager relationships. However, thanks to the new provisions set out in the GDPR, today's smart workers have new tools to help them become vigilant in the face of location and biometric data gathering and to protect themselves via collective bargaining and co-determination activities. The foundations for the Regulation make it quite clear that:

> (71): The data subject has the right not to be subject to a decision, which may include a measure, evaluating personal aspects relating to him or her which is based solely on automated processing and which produces legal effects concerning him or her or similarly significantly affects him

> or her, such as ... e-recruiting practices without any human intervention. Such processing includes profiling that consists of any form of automated processing of personal data evaluating the personal aspects of a natural person, in particular to analyse or predict aspects concerning the data subject's performance at work ... reliability or behaviour, location or movements, where it produces legal effects concerning him or her or similarly significantly affects him or her.

The GDPR is written with the individual as its focal subject. However, data collection operates at more levels than the individual and will impact groups of all kinds, qualities and quantities. Data governance should thus be seen as a collective good, in which all social partners must be involved. The bigger the dataset, the more powerful it is, because it can be used to train algorithms for decision-making. Therefore, responses to large datasets and their collection should not be individualised but should be *collective*. Consent is usually perceived to be a unidirectional arrangement and considered intrinsically impossible in the employment relationship. However, in countries which enjoy co-determination rights, digital workspace transformations require negotiation and bargaining between workers and management to proceed, and therefore must be collectively governed rather than only individually consented.

In this light, precise identification of the necessity for technological tracking must be part of worker/employer negotiations about what can be deemed proportional to workers' privacy and taking their wider interests seriously. Privacy is more than an interest, it is a right, but there are a whole range of interests surrounding and entangled with aspects of privacy which are at stake in the monitored workplace, which have relevance for discussions of necessity and proportionality. Privacy and related worker interests should be discussed and agreed in consultation and collective bargaining with unions. All monitoring and tracking processes must be made transparent to workers, with Data Protection Officers and trained trade union representatives working together to agree on proportionality and necessity.

CONCLUSION

Against this backdrop, it is not sensible to assume that technologies entering workplaces is part of 'business as usual'. The mirror for AI is repositioning, but this still reflects human behaviour and has significance for relations of production and their correspondent working conditions for the smart worker, including the AI trainer. The relations of production associated with specific forms of intelligence in digitalised, AI-augmented workspaces mostly reflect the standard employment relationship. The corresponding legislation, while offering some capacity for augmented collective bargaining, does not function to overturn these strictures. Smart workers should remain vigilant and aware of the structure within which AI activities are carried out, realising that the history of AI falls within this structure, and that the understanding of what makes an intelligent/smart machine, or an intelligent/smart human, is no fait accompli. Smart workers today will be those who use the types of intelligence ascribed to machines, such as collaborative or assistive capabilities, to collaborate with and assist each other in ways that facilitate a democratic workplace. Potentially, technologies can be appropriated and repurposed to overcome the hegemony of competition and growth models that impact the digitalised employment relationship.

While some policy characteristics within AI refer to *meaningful consent*, there are perhaps better possibilities for *meaningful dissent*. For example, co-determination could operate to at least facilitate democratic social relations around the possible violations of privacy rights. Most of the EU's post-Brexit members enjoy some kind of co-determination in both state-run firms and the private sector. The countries which do not enjoy the right to co-determination are Belgium, Bulgaria, Cyprus, Estonia, Italy, Latvia, Lithuania and Romania. To provide a platform for meaningful dissent at this stage, all EU member countries should implement some form of co-determination. In countries where this already exists, all data collection and processing activity should ideally be co-determined. Companies and labour authorities must take note of the legal apparatuses in countries with co-determination rights and ensure they are adhered to.

Another possible avenue for meaningful dissent is as follows: If workers had access to all the data that is being gathered about them – as they should, given the GDPR requirements – then smart workers and AI trainers could be empowered by accessing new forms of data that would help them identify areas for improvement, stimulate personal development, achieve higher levels of engagement, as well as identify data that is potentially discriminatory and then challenge this through collective bargaining. The data could be used by worker representatives and workers themselves to secure better pay – for example, if they could prove they consistently worked overtime – or to demonstrate the need for time off based on data relating to sickness or stress. With access to data about their work patterns, workers and their representatives could also negotiate with employers in areas of the employment relationship where they had not done so before. On the basis that numbers don't lie, overtime could be remunerated appropriately, sick leave taken seriously, and discrimination and stress avoided, allowing connections to be made between sickness levels and working conditions that are exacerbated in the AI-augmented workspace.

This issue has become more pressing than ever in the context of the Covid-19 pandemic, where labour processes are being reorganised at high speed with the help of digital technologies. In this situation, it is important for labour scholars to ask: Which forms of 'intelligence' will dominate the design and execution of AI-augmented tools and applications in the workplace? Will the worker be expected not just to mirror that intelligence, but also to train AI itself, according to the fundamental requirement of AI which is to provide and cultivate databases, through the affective labour of ghost work in content moderation and data service work? In this context, who is a 'smart worker' expected to be now, given the rise of smart machines? Who will the smart(est) worker need to be in the coming years, given the rise in AI in the workplace?

REFERENCES

Aloisi, A. and Gramano, E. (2019). Artificial Intelligence is Watching You At Work: Digital Surveillance, Employee Monitoring and Regulatory Issues in the EU Context. *Comparative Labour Law and Policy Journal* 41(1), 95–122. Special Issue: 'Automation, Artificial Intelligence and Labour Law', edited by V. De Stefano.

Anwar, M. A. and Graham, M. (2019). Digital Labour at Economic Margins: African Workers and the Global Information Economy. *Review of African Political Economy*. At https://ssrn.com/abstract=3499706.

D'Cruz, P. and Noronha, E. (2018). Target Experiences of Workplace Bullying on Online Labour Markets: Uncovering the Nuances of Resilience. *Employee Relations* 40(1), 139–54.

Delponte, L. (2018). *European Artificial Intelligence Leadership, the Path for an Integrated Vision*. Brussels: Policy Department for Economic, Scientific and Quality of Life Policies, European Parliament.

Dreyfus, H. (1979). *What Computers Can't Do*. New York: MIT Press.

European Commission (2018). Communication on Artificial Intelligence for Europe. Brussels: European Commission. At https://ec.europa.eu/digital-single-market/en/news/communication-artificial-intelligence-europe.

European Commission (2020). On Artificial Intelligence: A European Approach to Excellence and Trust. White Paper. At https://webcache.googleusercontent.com/search?q=cache:VR6rVqV3V_4J:https://ec.europa.eu/info/sites/info/files/commission-white-paper-artificial-intelligence-feb2020_en.pdf+&cd=1&hl=en&ct=clnk&gl=uk&client=firefox-b-d.

European Data Protection Board (EDPB) (2020). Guidelines 05/2020 on Consent Under Regulation 2016/679 Version 1.1. Adopted on May 2020.

Facebook (2020). Computer Vision. At https://ai.facebook.com/research/computer-vision.

Gillespie, T. (2018). *Custodians of the Internet: Platforms, Content Moderation, and the Hidden Decisions That Shape Social Media*. New Haven: Yale University Press.

Google (2019). Google Vision API (Part 13) – Detect Explicit Content (Safe Search Feature). At https://learndataanalysis.org/google-vision-api-part-13-detect-explicit-content-safe-search-feature.

Gray, Mary L. (2019). Ghost Work and the Future of Employment. Microsoft Research, 11 June 2019. EmTech Next. At https://events.technologyreview.com/video/watch/mary-gray-microsoft-ghost-work.

Gray, M. L. and Suri, S. (2019). *Ghost Work: How to Stop Silicon Valley from Building a New Global Underclass*. New York: Mariner.

Hutter, M. (2012). One Decade of Universal Artificial Intelligence. In Pei Want and Ben Goertzel, eds. *Theoretical Foundations of Artificial General Intelligence*, Vol. 4. Amsterdam: Atlantis, 67–88.

IDC and Open Evidence (2017). *The European Data Market Study*. At https://datalandscape.eu/study-reports/european-data-market-study-final-report.

Levin, S. (2017). Google to Hire Thousands of Moderators After Outcry Over YouTube Abuse Videos. *Guardian*, 4 December. At www.theguardian.com/technology/2017/dec/04/google-youtube-hire-moderators-child-abuse-videos.

Malabou, C. (2015). Post-Trauma: Towards a New Definition?, in M. Pasquinelli, ed. *Alleys of Your Mind: Augmented Intelligence and its Traumas*. Lüneburg: Meson Press, 187–98.

Marx, K. (1993). *Grundrisse*. London: Penguin.

Microsoft Azure (2020). Content Moderator. At https://azure.microsoft.com/en-us/services/cognitive-services/content-moderator.

Moore, P. (2018a). *The Quantified Self in Precarity: Work, Technology and What Counts*. London and New York: Routledge.

Moore, P. (2018b). Tracking Affective Labour for Agility in the Quantified Workplace. *Body & Society* 24(3): 39–67.

Moore, P. V. (2020). The Mirror for (Artificial) Intelligence: In Whose Reflection? *Comparative Labour Law and Policy Journal* 41(1), 47–67. Special Issue: 'Automation, Artificial Intelligence and Labour Law', edited by V. De Stefano.

Newton, C. (2019). The Trauma Floor: The Secret Lives of Facebook Moderators in America. The Verge. Online: www.theverge.com/2019/2/25/18229714/cognizant-facebook-content-moderator-interviews-trauma-working-conditions-arizona.

Noronha, E. and D'Cruz, P. (2009). *Employee Identity in Indian Call Centres: The Notion of Professionalism*. New Delhi: Sage/Response.

Organisation for Economic Cooperation and Development (OECD) (2019). Recommendation of the Council on Artificial Intelligence. OECD, LEGAL/0449, 12 May 2019. At https://legalinstruments.oecd.org/en/instruments/OECD-LEGAL-0449.

Pasquinelli, M., ed. (2015). *Alleys of Your Mind: Augmented Intelligence and its Traumas*. Lüneburg: Meson Press.

Perel, M. and Elkin-Korean, N. (2017). Black Box Tinkering: Beyond Disclosure in Algorithmic Enforcement. *Florida Law Review* 69, 181–222.

Pinto, A. T. (2015). The Pigeon in the Machine: The Concept of Control in Behaviourism and Cybernetics, in M. Pasquinelli, ed. *Alleys of Your Mind: Augmented Intelligence and its Traumas*. Lüneburg: Meson Press, 23–36.

Punsmann, B. G. (2018). Three Months in Hell. What I Learned from Three Months of Content Moderation for Facebook in Berlin. At https://sz-magazin.sueddeutsche.de/internet/three-months-in-hell-84381.

Ruckenstein, M. and Turunen, L. (2019). Re-humanizing the Platform: Content Moderators and the Logic of Care, *New Media and Society* 22(6), 1026–42.

Sewell, G. (2005). Nice work? Rethinking Managerial Control in an Era of Knowledge Work. *Organization* 12(5), 685–704.

Wong, Q. (2019). Content Moderators Protect Facebook's 2.3 Billion Members. Who Protects Them? Net News. At www.cnet.com/news/facebook-content-moderation-is-an-ugly-business-heres-who-does-it.

World Bank (2015). The Global Opportunity in Online Outsourcing. At http://documents.worldbank.org/curated/en/138371468000900555/The-global-opportunity-in-online-outsourcing.

2

Work Now, Profit Later: AI Between Capital, Labour and Regulation

Toni Prug and Paško Bilić

Actors promoting artificial intelligence preach a one-directional technological evolution. They argue that societies on the cutting edge of digital innovation should follow a process of systemic change from data-dependent services to data-fed, autonomous and intelligent systems. The field of current and future AI application ranges from web search, news filtering, credit scoring and banking services, facial recognition, machine learning microchips, network optimisation and autonomous vehicles, to advanced healthcare biometrics, drug discovery, welfare benefits and other government assessment, cyber-threat hunting, anti-counterfeiting, music mastering and crop monitoring. Development of commercial systems requires substantial capital and labour expenditures. Yet the market value for many AI products and services is uncertain. The final output is not a commodity, as one would expect from a Marxian perspective. Instead, such expenditures usually result in forms of intellectual property rights (e.g. patents) that provide legal ownership of future economic returns. AI develops under future-oriented thinking and a logic of postponement, often utilising services provided to users free of charge and enabling contributions outside of the firm, such as in free and open source production. Economic gains, social benefits and democratic oversight are all pushed forward to an unknown point in time, somewhere down the risky AI production line. Capital gains a first-mover advantage, while labour and society need to catch up and adapt to the consequences of capital expansion, or capital losses and market crashes.

To address some of these points, this chapter is organised as follows. In the first section, we discuss AI-related activities of the largest IT companies. An outline of the growing schism between the varied types of labour, based on the complexity of tasks performed and the growing issue of invisibility of labour within AI systems, follows. The final section discusses AI regulation, contrasting the AI firms' claims on their ethical principles with the realities of capitalist production.

EXPANDING CAPITAL

Concentration and centralisation of capital is one of the key mechanisms in capitalism, going back to industrial times in what Marx (1996) described as a process in which 'larger capitals always beat the smaller'. There are many advantages of concentrated and centralised capital. It can sustain losses in some operating areas longer. It can absorb risks from market fluctuations and low demand to starve competition. It can reinvest parts of capital to develop and produce new commodities. It can supply markets with constantly differentiated and updated commodities. It can use accumulated capital to acquire and merge competing companies. It can influence political and regulatory processes. As Harvey noted cynically: '[capital] prefers certainties, the quiet life and the possibility of leisurely and cautious changes that go with a monopolistic style of working and living outside of the rough and tumble of competition' (2014: 139, 140). Technological innovation adds a layer of uncertainty as it is not clear if spending on salaries, research and development, and commercialisation will provide returns. If there is a lack of markets to absorb new commodities, the problems for capital multiply as capital circulation and accumulation come to a stall. Monopoly is a structural position that allows capital to mitigate risks and control innovation in order to keep expanding and growing.

Artificial intelligence promises to be a generic technology with cross-industry applications. The first to jump on the bandwagon are private equity funds and venture capitalists looking for the next big thing to shower with cash. More than $50 billion was invested in AI start-ups between 2011 and 2018, two thirds of which was invested in the United States (OECD 2018). At the same time, only 10 per cent of venture capital funded start-ups reported any revenue between 2013 and 2016 (Bughin et al. 2017: 3). Global tech giants such as Google and Baidu have spent between $20 and 30 billion in 2016 alone, 90 per cent of which went on research and development, and 10 per cent on acquisitions (Bughin et al. 2017: 6). GAFAM (Google, Amazon, Facebook, Apple and Microsoft) spent more than $70 billion on research and development in 2017. However, despite their aggressive marketing, the social benefits are questionable. Think of quotes such as this one from Microsoft's AI team: 'The era of artificial intelligence is upon us and has the potential to transform our lives, industries and society in ways that may be difficult to imagine today' (Azizirad 2018). Underneath the ideological layer, there are clear economic incentives dictated by the character of capitalist production and national and international social and market conditions. Advancements in AI can improve corporate productivity and efficiency and provide solutions that can be applied across industry sectors. This provides new impetus to capital accumulation and corporate growth.

Outputs of massive investments in research and development are visible in the type and number of patents by GAFAM. There is an ongoing race in patent application in areas such as artificial intelligence, autonomous vehicles, cybersecurity and healthcare (CBInsights 2017). Of course, pumping dollars into R&D and applying for patents does not guarantee anything if it does not result in commodities exchanged in the market. GAFAM also engage in mergers and acquisitions to scoop up skilled labour and new ideas and to reduce risks of capital losses. Between 2010 and August 2019, Apple made 20 acquisitions, Google 14, Microsoft 10, Facebook 8, and Amazon 7 in the field of AI (CBInsights 2019).

DIVIDING AND HIDING LABOUR

In order to create value from AI, capital requires skilled labour in machine learning, artificial neural networks, natural language processing, logistics regression, and so on. One of the unique features of capitalism is that labour becomes a commodity within the capitalist production and that new technical discoveries constantly create new markets for new skills. Yet capital is also in a struggle to reduce costs, improve efficiency, increase productivity and speed up capital accumulation at the expense of labour. This is one of the main contradictions of capitalism. Currently, AI skills are in high demand and giant tech companies are trying to attract talent with high salaries, bonuses and stock-based compensations (SBCs). Usually SBCs come with a vested period for new employees, which means they can only exercise their stock options after a certain period. This creates an effective mechanism for attracting, retaining and managing labour. SBCs align workers' interests with the economic performance of the company. GAFAM companies spent between 2.1 per cent (Apple) and 9.1 per cent (Facebook) of their 2017 revenue on stock-based compensations. Translated to US dollars, this amounts to 3.64 billion for Facebook and 4.81 billion for Apple.[1] The bulk of this, however, goes to top tier management and ownership.

Reports on how AI will add new economic value and increase declining productivity rates caused by ageing populations and low birth rates are becoming widespread (Manyika and Sneader 2018). At the same time, there is growing dissatisfaction among tech workers in the US with issues ranging from poor management, long working hours, salary disparities, racism and sexism to ethical concerns over cooperation with radical politics and non-democratic regimes (Tech Workers Coalition 2018). Mergers and acquisitions are a way for capital to add new skills, replenish existing labour and replace obsolete workers. Creating demand for new AI skills puts pressure on nation states to adapt to the needs of the market and to introduce educational reforms focusing on STEM research and digital skills. While skilled labour is in high demand and leading technical universities are racing to provide new cohorts of talent, low-skilled labour is in high supply due to the distributed nature of digital networks and the availability of micro-tasks worldwide. As Huws (2014) argues, technologically driven capitalism always requires a new division of labour which results in parallel processes of reskilling and deskilling.

GAFAM have been particularly active in outsourcing micro-tasks for improving their technical systems, performing machine learning activities and manual content evaluations. Armies of globally dispersed, work-at-home, part-time wage-labourers perform search engine evaluations (Bilić 2016), moderate offensive and abusive content on social media (Roberts 2016, 2018), and perform different tasks through Amazon's Mechanical Turk. As Irani notes, 'the dreams of AI have become more urgent as Web 2.0 businesses attempt to amass and extract value from increasing volumes of people's data' (2015b: 724). Machine learning algorithms require training based on datasets classified by humans. The study of working conditions of 3,500 workers living in 75 countries found that despite 'micro-workers' being necessary for the AI results to appear magically automated, workers and their jobs remain invisible, poorly regulated and paid, seemingly not directly employed by the corporations that construct and run such systems (Berg et al. 2018; Irani 2015a). As long as this type of labour remains hidden

1. Sources: SEC Form 10K filings.

and left to unregulated markets, AI developments will push the division of labour to the extreme, with a handful of corporate owners and top brass management capturing a larger slice of income at the expense of labour. Profits from inflated intangible and financial asset value will be concentrated at the top. These labourers will be left outside of the world of technological plenty to struggle with invisible employers, algorithmic surveillance, platform management and lack of collective bargaining. More initiatives such as Fairwork (Graham and Woodcock 2018) will be needed to make the global labour supply chains visible and to make platforms and future AI systems more accountable. While the EU has made initial large-scale studies and positive recommendations aimed at regulating hidden digital labour and providing it with currently missing social protections (Forde et al. 2017: 13–14), a system of transnational coordination and regulation will be required to capture the slippery power of global capital built around data commodification and hidden human labour.

ESCAPING REGULATION

Promises of productivity and economic gains from AI development have captured the imagination of an impressive range of transnational organisations and nation states.[2] The gold rush mentality is evident in policy documents and strategic reports that promise to harness AI and provide future benefits. The competitive race for AI dominance fuels a geopolitical struggle largely driven by investments in the United States and state support in China. The EU is trying to catch up and find a unique edge between these opposite poles (EU 2018b). The debates on regulation of AI have been mostly confined to policy-making specialists. The exception is weapons, where AI regulation has commanded some public profile due to the obvious dangers inherent in such automated systems.[3] Utilisation of AI can have significant consequences for both individuals (not being granted a

2. A large number of countries, including the USA, the UK, France and China, have strategies and sometimes legal frameworks to deal with some aspects of AI. See the large institutional actors' frameworks: OECD 2019; G20 2019; EU 2018a.

3. Initially more than 1,000 experts and robotics engineers signed an open letter asking for a ban on offensive autonomous weapons (Gibbs 2015). The list grew and has since attracted over 4,000 expert signatures in the form of an open letter to the UN (Petitioners 2017).

loan, welfare assistance rejected)[4] and broader social affairs (news filtering, injecting false news, espionage). AI regulation has proven to be difficult thus far due to its novelty and its opaque character stemming primarily from AI's ubiquity and technological complexity and from accentuated competitiveness among producers resulting from the potential rewards for those who capture and construct new areas of the AI market early. The most obvious question that arises is how can we regulate the behaviour of technologies whose internal workings are often inaccessible, or can be only understood by the most highly skilled engineers in the field?

A recent approach proposed by 23 scientists in the journal *Nature* is to study machine behaviour in the context of its environment, which includes other machines, humans, socially constructed objects and the rules they interact with (Rahwan et al. 2019). Studying how machines act, the authors emphasise repeatedly, can only be done by interdisciplinary efforts. However, the makers of those machines – mathematicians, engineers and computer scientists – are too close to the object of study and lack the skills necessary to do it alone. Machines, the authors warn, 'operate within a larger socio-technical fabric', and it is 'their human stakeholders that are ultimately responsible for any harm their deployment might cause' (Rahwan et al. 2019: 483). The economic context gets only a few mentions in the article: 'economic forces can have indirect but substantial effects on the behaviours exhibited by machines' (Rahwan et al. 2019: 481). While it is clearly stated that the mechanism by which the more sophisticated algorithms learn 'depends on both an algorithm and its environment', economic aspects, the driving forces of production, are left out of consideration in any meaningful detail on either a micro or macro level. No monetary aspects considering either profits or public investment get a mention, despite profit-making being the driving logic of capitalist economies. The only time when maximising criteria for algorithms appear is to point out that in trading programs, 'more sophisticated agents may compute strategies based on ... explicit maximization of expected utility' (Rahwan et al. 2019: 480). And yet both utility, the central category of the mainstream economic approach, and its

4. A vast number of examples are scattered across the sources referenced in this chapter, with the AI Now Institute at the forefront of such reporting. One instance with a large number of people affected was when algorithm-based decision-making on student visas proved to be error prone, leading to unjustified deportations of students from the UK (Sonnad 2018).

re-conceptualisations[5] have been the subject of intense criticisms for over a century. The most problematic aspect has been its entirely deductive and analytical character devoid of any empirical referent, lacking measurability and empirical verifiability (Lewin 1996: 1311; Mirowski and Hands 1998). This is an area where sociological, anthropological and political economy approaches can introduce a set of questions and research directions, steering the debate towards macro and micro parameters that the social and economic forces operate within, from interests of national economies and accumulation of capital, to emphasis on labour and its historically difficult yet symbiotic relationship with capital and national economic development, all of it often intertwined in the selection of the type and size of public production and its investments.

The AI annual report by New York University focuses on accountability, the question of responsibility for the harm caused by AI. The following challenges were placed at the forefront: 'growing accountability gap in AI, which favours those who create and deploy such technologies at the expense of those most affected'; 'use of surveillance ... increasing the potential for centralised control and oppression'; 'increasing government use of automated decision systems that directly impact individuals and communities without established accountability structures' (Whittaker, Crawford, Dobbe et al. 2018: 7). The report documents how governments' increasing use of AI, provided on many occasions by Google and Amazon (Rekognition tool), has been found to be prone to errors, with racial bias in face recognition leading to life-altering government decisions, such as prison detention (2018: 15–16). Setting up ethical rules and advisory boards – a corporate self-regulatory mechanism with a poor historical record – has been found to be ineffective (2018: 30–1). That Google has been developing a more explicitly censored version of its search for the Chinese market – relying extensively on AI, thus breaking its own AI principles (Pichai 2018) – the report documents, comes as no surprise. Google, like any other capitalist firm, operates by chasing profit, not according to written codes of conduct

5. From the late nineteenth century, the earliest days of what we know as neoclassical economics today, economists were acutely aware of the problems of measurability of their central concept, utility. Some hoped it would be resolved in the future with the availability of better data (Stanley Jevons, Leon Walras, among the earliest authors, and Robert Solow more recently in 1997), while others tried to replace utility with concepts that would not be open to the same criticisms (Wilfred Pareto with indifference curves, Paul Samuelson with revealed preferences) – all without success thus far.

without legal binding. Similar to the focus on public interest and accountability in the use of algorithms, and present in a more comprehensive EU study (Koene et al. 2019), the AI Now report makes some bold recommendations. It asks AI companies to 'waive trade secrecy and other legal claims that would prevent algorithmic accountability in the public sector', since 'government and public institutions must be able to understand and explain how and why decisions are made', it being imperative 'that the balance of power shifts back in the public's favour' (Whittaker, Crawford, Dobbe et al. 2018: 42).[6]

Yet, judging by the history of financial regulation in the USA, the notion of public interest has historically been deployed in regulatory laws to counter markets more as a rhetorical device than an actual basis for regulation (Sylla 1996). At best, the concept of public interest has an ambiguous character in the minds of creators of regulatory laws (Keller and Gehlmann 1988: 338), with a more pessimistic reading seeing it as a derivative from the interests of market actors, serving 'efficiency, competition and capital formation' (Huber 2016: 419). In this light, appeals to ethics and public interest demonstrate a lack of understanding of the driving force behind government and public sector activities. The use of public interest as a proxy for the unspecified logic of non-profit productive activities remains a problematic proposition for the utilisation of AI beyond the capitalist logic that necessarily dominates the orientation of research and development in GAFAM and other leading companies in the sector.[7]

CONCLUSION

Autonomous machines easily capture the public imagination and provide a technological imaginary manipulated for the economic purposes of new wealth creation. Concentrated and centralised capital has a first-mover advantage in harnessing the potential market value of future products and services. Acting from a monopolistic position provides many opportunities for absorbing risks. With enormous capital and labour resources, in addition

6. For a set of more concrete, practical and operational recommendations see Reisman et al. 2018, and the excellent *Algorithmic Accountability Policy Toolkit* (Anon 2018).

7. While we know what drives production under capital (accumulation of capital), what its direct aims are and its measures of success (surplus value, appearing in forms of profit), the same cannot be said for non-profit activities.

to favourable regulatory interventions, GAFAM can easily lead the charge in AI development. However, what is certain is that AI will not do away with some of the main contradictions of capitalism, including the central one between capital and labour. Moreover, it will likely create a more volatile environment, driven by the logic of postponement and future-oriented thinking. The logic of market adoption and profit extraction is currently in a good position to impose itself over issues concerning workers and work processes, such as equality, social benefits and democratic oversight. New divisions of labour will occur, new skills will be deployed, and part-time workers will be exploited to feed the increasing data hunger of AI systems. The record of accomplishment of GAFAM has not been stellar, to say the least, in these areas. The opaque character of algorithms and algorithmic-driven systems lends itself poorly to regulation, aiding the interest of unhindered capital accumulation while hindering democratic oversight and regulation. Leaving the development of future technologies such as AI in the hands of capital alone promises more perils down the road. Exposing the new divisions and obfuscations of labour, new forms of commodification and the complexities of AI-driven production, is necessary to open up those areas to worker collective action and to democratic regulation.

REFERENCES

Anon (2018). *Algorithmic Accountability Policy Toolkit*. At https://ainowinstitute.org/aap-toolkit.pdf.

Azizirad, M. (2018). Microsoft AI: Empowering Transformation. Microsoft AI Blog. At https://blogs.microsoft.com/ai/microsoft-ai-empowering-transformation.

Berg, J. et al. (2018). *Digital Labour Platforms and the Future of Work: Towards Decent Work in the Online World*. At www.ilo.org/global/publications/books/WCMS_645337/lang--en/index.htm.

Bilić, P. (2016). Search Algorithms, Hidden Labour and Information Control. *Big Data & Society* 3(1). At https://doi.org/10.1177/2053951716652159.

Bughin, J. et al. (2017). *Artificial Intelligence: The Next Digital Frontier?* At www.mckinsey.com/~/media/McKinsey/Industries/Advanced%20Electronics/Our%20Insights/How%20artificial%20intelligence%20can%20deliver%20real%20value%20to%20companies/MGI-Artificial-Intelligence-Discussion-paper.ashx.

CBInsights (2017). *Winners And Losers in the Patent Wars Between Amazon, Google, Facebook, Apple, and Microsoft*. At www.cbinsights.com/research/innovation-patents-apple-google-amazon-facebook-expert-intelligence.

CBInsights (2019). *The Race for AI: Here Are the Tech Giants Rushing to Snap Up Artificial Intelligence Startups*. At www.cbinsights.com/research/innovation-patents-apple-google-amazon-facebook-expert-intelligence.

EU (2018a). *Artificial Intelligence for Europe*. At https://eur-lex.europa.eu/legal-content/EN/TXT/?uri=COM:2018:237:FIN.

EU (2018b). *The Age of Artificial Intelligence: Towards a European Strategy for Human-Centric Machines*. At https://ec.europa.eu/jrc/communities/en/community/digitranscope/document/age-artificial-intelligence-towards-european-strategy-human-centric.

Forde, C. et al. (2017). *The Social Protection of Workers in the Platform Economy*. At www.europarl.europa.eu/RegData/etudes/STUD/2017/614184/IPOL_STU(2017)614184_EN.pdf.

G20 (2019). G20 Ministerial Statement on Trade and Digital Economy. At http://trade.ec.europa.eu/doclib/press/index.cfm?id=2027.

Gibbs, S. (2015). Musk, Wozniak and Hawking Urge Ban on Warfare AI and Autonomous Weapons. *Guardian*, 27 July. At www.theguardian.com/technology/2015/jul/27/musk-wozniak-hawking-ban-ai-autonomous-weapons.

Graham, M. and Woodcock, J. (2018). Towards a Fairer Platform Economy: Introducing the Fairwork Foundation. *Alternate Routes* 29, 242–53.

Harvey, D. (2014). *Seventeen Contradictions and the End of Capitalism*. Oxford and New York: Oxford University Press.

Huber, W. D. (2016). The Myth of Protecting the Public Interest: The Case of the Missing Mandate in Federal Securities Law. *Journal of Business & Securities Law* 16(2), 401–23.

Huws, U. (2014). *Labor in the Global Digital Economy: The Cybertariat Comes of Age*. New York: Monthly Review Press.

Irani, L. (2015a). Justice for 'Data Janitors'. At www.publicbooks.org/justice-for-data-janitors.

Irani, L. (2015b). The Cultural Work of Microwork. *New Media & Society* 17(5), 720–39.

Keller, E. and Gehlmann, G. A. (1988). Introductory Comment: A Historical Introduction to the Securities Act of 1933 and the Securities Exchange Act of 1934 Symposium: Current Issues in Securities Regulation. *Ohio State Law Journal* 49, 329–352.

Koene, A. et al. (2019). *A Governance Framework for Algorithmic Accountability and Transparency: Study*. At www.europarl.europa.eu/RegData/etudes/STUD/2019/624262/EPRS_STU(2019)624262_EN.pdf.

Lewin, S. B. (1996). Economics and Psychology: Lessons for Our Own Day from the Early Twentieth Century. *Journal of Economic Literature* 34(3), 1293–323.

Manyika, J. and Sneader, K. (2018). AI, Automation, and the Future of Work: Ten Things to Solve For. At www.mckinsey.com/featured-insights/future-of-work/ai-automation-and-the-future-of-work-ten-things-to-solve-for.

Marx, K. (1996). *Capital: Vol. 1*. Collected Works 35. London: Lawrence & Wishart.

Mirowski, P. and Hands, W. (1998). A Paradox of Budgets: The Postwar Stabilization of American Neoclassical Demand Theory. In M. Morgan and M. Rutherford, eds, *From Interwar Pluralism to Postwar Neoclassicism*. Durham, NC: Duke University Press, 260–89.

OECD (2018). Private Equity Investment in Artificial Intelligence. At www.oecd.org/going-digital/ai/private-equity-investment-in-artificial-intelligence.pdf.

OECD (2019). Recommendation of the Council on Artificial Intelligence. At https://legalinstruments.oecd.org/en/instruments/OECD-LEGAL-0449.

Petitioners (2017). An Open Letter to the United Nations Convention on Certain Conventional Weapons. At https://futureoflife.org/autonomous-weapons-open-letter-2017.

Pichai, S. (2018). AI at Google: Our Principles. At https://blog.google/technology/ai/ai-principles.

Rahwan, I. et al. (2019). Machine Behaviour. *Nature* 568(7753), 477–86.

Reisman, D., Schultz, J. Crawford, K. and Whittaker, M. (2018). *Algorithmic Impact Assessments: A Practical Framework for Public Agency Accountability*. At https://ainowinstitute.org/aiareport2018.pdf.

Roberts, S. T. (2016). Commercial Content Moderation: Digital Labourers' Dirty Work. *Media Studies Publications* 12. At https://ir.lib.uwo.ca/commpub/12.

Roberts, S. T. (2018). Digital Detritus: 'Error' and the Logic of Opacity in Social Media Content Moderation. *First Monday* 23(3). At https://firstmonday.org/ojs/index.php/fm/article/view/8283.

Sonnad, N. (2018). A Flawed Algorithm Led the UK to Deport Thousands of Students. *Quartz*, 3 May. At https://qz.com/1268231/a-toeic-test-led-the-uk-to-deport-thousands-of-students.

Sylla, R. (1996). The 1930s Financial Reforms in Historical Perspective. In Dimitri Papadimitriou, ed. *Stability in the Financial System*. Basingstoke: Palgrave Macmillan, 13–25.

Tech Workers Coalition (2018). Tech Workers, Platform Workers, and Workers' Inquiry. At https://notesfrombelow.org/article/tech-workers-platform-workers-and-workers-inquiry.

Whittaker, M., Crawford, K., Dobbe, R. et al. (2018). *AI Now Report 2018*. At https://ainowinstitute.org/AI_Now_2018_Report.pdf.

3
Delivering Food on Bikes: Between Machinic Subordination and Autonomy in the Algorithmic Workplace

Benjamin Herr

Algorithms are consciously constructed and implemented in the capitalist labour process to discipline and control labour. They are embedded in the use of rating tools, on-by-data extraction and tracking technologies, all of it fostering managerial surveillance and thereby facilitating labour extraction (Gandini 2018; Srnicek 2017; Woodcock 2020). It is argued that this quantification of labour in algorithmic workplaces leads to higher alienation among workers (Moore 2018). So, one might argue that the use of algorithms could facilitate 'breaking' these subordinated groups, as workers face the blank logic of the capitalist labour process. But what if it does not always work this way? What if workers' perceptions are shaped by aspects other than feeling like a tool for profit production?

This chapter gives 'priority to empirical research that looks at how people experience capitalism' (Moore 2018: 127). It does so by investigating a platform company in the food-delivery sector that relies on automated dispatching and subsequent use of algorithms for running the labour process (Herr 2017, 2018). It asks how workers perceive their work in an attempt to assess the relevance of the algorithmic workplace in their narratives, claiming that such an understanding is an important yet overlooked starting point for any project aiming for working-class power.

MACHINIC SUBORDINATION OR AUTONOMY IN THE ALGORITHMIC WORKPLACE?

Broadly, a Marxist notion of technology in the capitalist labour process highlights its use for capital accumulation. This could either be because technology increases productivity and workers produce relatively more in a given time, or because technology fosters control over the pace and activities of workers (Marx 1962: 492). In the section of *Capital* on 'Machinery and Large-Scale Industry', Marx describes the deskilling that accompanies the rise of the factory system. Technology transforms social relations in the labour process to the extent that machines subordinate replaceable workers. Insisting that technology is not neutral, Marx argues that it is instead an instrument of class struggle, transforming and stabilising relations of exploitation, where the particular appliance of technology reduces living labour to an appendage of the machine. This idea is taken up by French philosophers Deleuze and Guattari (2005). They offer a concept that can be rephrased as *machinic subordination*. Here, they aim to grasp the nature and reproduction of power relations in current modes of capitalist exploitation. The concept focuses on the subordination of human bodies to serve a larger productive mechanism. The degradation of human bodies to components of a machine furthers the abstraction of human labour. Deleuze and Guattari argue that the growing importance of postindustrial work for capitalist accumulation, together with developments in new technology and artificial intelligence in particular, develop 'an entire system of machinic enslavement' (2005: 505). The subject does not make use of the machine, rather, the machine uses subjects to fulfil the conditions for profit production. This follows a tendency in capitalist employment relations to increase the interchangeability of workers (Horkheimer and Adorno 2006), where machinic subordination turns humans and machines into interchangeable parts of the labour process, in order to extend surplus value (Lazzarato 2014).

Looking at capital's contemporary quest for relative surplus value, we see the use of artificial intelligence as a means that ensures class subordination, obscures class relations and quantifies human labour in novel ways (Moore 2018). In platform food-delivery for instance, the app is the point of production (Gandini 2018). It exercises detailed control over the labour process (Edwards 1986: 6) through managing the orders and required delivery time, intentionally reducing workers' discretion to a minimum to increase interchangeability. This empirically reflects the arguments of Marx and Deleuze and Guattari about the relationship of technology and human labour in labour processes designed for the pursuit of profit production.

Platform delivery workers have little knowledge of algorithms' functioning (Goods, Veen and Barratt 2019). Indeed, the very construction of algorithms hampers workers' autonomy (Shapiro 2018), and the technology applied in the labour process furthers control via monitoring and rating (Gandini 2018). However, job quality is a multidimensional space, with its contradictory nature and inherent tensions, where workers' perceptions of their jobs are not necessarily shaped solely by the use of algorithms (Goods, Veen and Barratt 2019). Subjectively enjoyable work elements cover more than the algorithmic dispatching. The work is also about social interactions, about cycling, and about being outside.

This reflects what Austrian sociologist Marie Jahoda (1982) argued for in her social-psychological conception of work. While acknowledging the analytical perspective that points to the exploitative character of work in the context of capital accumulation, Jahoda says that work also fulfils necessary psycho-social human needs, for instance the need for time structure or taking part in a larger collective effort. Closely related to this idea is the argument that many jobs allow for some degree of autonomy, without denying the exploitative character of work for capital. Work autonomy is defined as workers' control over their time and activities. This includes who decides on the pace of work, who decides on the time worked, who determines where tasks will be performed and who maintains discretion over the tasks performed (Tilly and Tilly 1998: 90). Giving workers discretion over some work tasks is identified as being a powerful tool to maintain consent in the workplace. Burowoy (1979, 1985) for instance describes how workers take part in management systems designed to exploit them. Friedman (1977) was the first to conceptualise workers' discretion over the labour process as a tool for control by the management. In what Friedman called *responsible autonomy*, workers tend to feel less alienated. This fosters general control, i.e. the accommodation of workers to the overall aims of the labour process (Edwards 1986: 6). What we see here is that even though workers might be put under managerial control, they could still feel an 'illusion of freedom' (Waters and Woodcock 2017).

In the context of bicycle delivery work, this should not be overlooked by critical social research. What bicycle delivery work requires is experience, even though the routing might be substituted by an app, as it is in the case of platform food-delivery. Bicycle couriers appropriate the city in a spontaneous and creative manner. Similar to Burawoy's (1979) workplace games, couriers play with urban spaces (Kidder 2009). Going from A to B using a bicycle in a space that is designed for motor vehicles fosters the couriers' tacit knowledge. This tacit knowledge not only includes a mental map of the city, with bypasses, fastest routes and so forth, but also the handling of the bicycle in the city traffic. This affects the individual's construction of autonomy and thereby impacts how workers perceive their work relationship (Fincham 2006). They might feel autonomous in their performance, even though they are controlled and poorly paid (Jaros 2005). We can assume a similar social dynamic in platform food-delivery. For instance, Griesbach et al., in their research on US platform food-deliverers, concluded that respondents valued the degree of autonomy offered by the platform. The platforms investigated 'do allow workers relative autonomy over when they work and what particular tasks they accept' (Griesbach et al. 2019: 13). However, this relative autonomy is conditioned, as it 'exists under algorithmic control, which includes incentive pricing, ratings, and incomplete information as well as the broader uncertainty and unpredictability of earnings' (Griesbach et al. 2019: 13). Platform delivery workers might have some discretion over the routing to the customer's location. Even though the app facilitates the navigation process, workers can use their own routes (Veen, Barratt and Goods 2019).

We are thus left with two perspectives: one highlighting the machinic subordination of workers, the other pointing to the relative autonomy possible in some jobs. Both perspectives impact workers and thus also the ways they might want to be involved in a political project that aims to restore working-class power. This chapter now asks how these perspectives might be articulated in the narratives of workers in an archetypical algorithmic workplace – a food-delivery platform company in Vienna, Austria.

THE APP IS THE BOSS

The purpose of the technology applied at the platform food-delivery company is to coordinate a high number of workers while restricting their discretion in fulfilling work tasks. An illustrative example is the so-called *double order*, i.e. two deliveries from the same restaurant. While the first delivery is received on time, the other may take longer. *Nick* is a 23-year-old foreign student who is a freelance worker. He complains about how the app handles these orders, because 'order A should be already at the customer's but you still have to wait for order B'. This is because workers can only see a customer's address after receiving the meal. If there are two deliveries, it is necessary to confirm both in the app in order to see the addresses of the customers. So, it is not possible to deliver the order that's ready, while the second one is still being prepared by the restaurant. Addresses are then only shown in the sequence planned by the algorithm. Workers cannot autonomously re-arrange orders, and this can result in a delayed drop-off and so affect the tip.

David criticises the particular use of technology as well. Being a trained milling cutter and having worked as a bicycle courier for many years, he is confronted with the standardised nature of task allocation in platform delivery. He elaborates on an example where, after he'd picked up an order, he had to go back to the same restaurant to wait for a following order:

> I should wait there for 10 minutes to deliver and I think to myself this is senseless. Instead I could deliver my first order and be back right on time. And if I would do it the way they [management] want to force me to do, I would have to wait for 30 minutes. But they do not take you seriously if you try to explain that to them.

Generally, he misses some sort of social closeness. At the platform 'you are just a dot that they track', not a human being. This contrasts with his earlier experiences in courier services, where he felt close to his fellow workers: 'this is something I know from many other messenger services, this is tremendously important. These personal relationships with each other.'

BEING YOUR OWN BOSS

As we can see, the app is central to organising the labour process at the platform food-delivery company. The app provides a hyperlink to Google Maps, which shows a route from the worker's location to the customer or restaurant. However, workers are not obliged to use it, resulting in three types of users within the workforce. First, there are those who find their route autonomously, relying on their own experience or street map. These most closely resemble the archetype of an urban bike messenger. Second, workers may use the Google Maps route but refrain from using the navigation system. Third, workers can use both and ride standardised and automated from delivery to delivery. *Tamino* is a worker of the third type.

Tamino is 19 years old and preparing for university entry exams. He lives at his parents' home and his income through the platform provides a 'bonus' for him. Tamino tells me that he uses not only the Google Maps route, but also the navigation system. The navigation system basically reduces you to a riding unit. As another worker once told me 'that's so awesome, I can completely shut off my brains'. Since Tamino represents the part of the workforce riding in the most automated way, I asked him if this does not make his workday a bit dull. He replied:

> No. From a technical aspect, yeah, it is dull, but traffic and the city are vibrant and in constant change, it continues on and on. You meet different people, every day, you see different streets, every day, different neighbourhoods, you get to know new restaurants, all that kind of stuff. This is what it makes so interesting to me.

Although the work tasks might be monotonous, the actual experience of the performance – navigating through the city – impacts the perception of the work as well. Algorithmic management might therefore not be the only force shaping workers' experience. Tamino gives us an excellent example to support this claim. On the one hand, his workday is defined by the automated dispatching of deliveries. On the other hand, he described aspects of the workday untouched by the form of dispatching and that shaped his perception of the job. An analysis of managerial control in an attempt to support working-class power therefore requires the inclusion of the experience of work.

Elias, on the other hand, represents the part of the workforce closer to the archetype of bike messengers. As an immigrant worker, the national labour legislation required him to find a job within four months of his arrival. Usually, a deliverer must work three months minimum as a freelancer until the platform will hire them as an employee. In Elias's case, he was hired as an employee right away. He became aware of the platform due to its 'street presence' and a 'fairly prominent hiring campaign'. He says that the job is one of the most satisfying he has had, because he does not have to be in an office. Elias tells us about his cycling background, and that cycling is for him the ultimate and best form of transportation. Generally, he thinks of the people working in this industry as being open-minded ('I guess it's the exercise'), which makes it very enjoyable for him to be part of. In addition, the social environment of the job offers a support structure for him as a foreigner. With regard to remuneration, Elias compares the delivery work at the platform with similar sectors, coming to the conclusion that 'as platform deliverers we are not as badly paid as people who ride bikes and deliver packages from A to B'.

Right at the beginning of our conversation he started to elaborate on the navigation, saying that the delivery job had helped him to get used to the city. At the beginning he used a pocket map to navigate, but 'after a certain point you need the experience of riding'. Elias vigorously rejects Google Maps, saying that 'no person that rides professionally takes the route that Google Maps tells you to take, because it is 9 times out of 10 ridiculous'. The experience of riding fosters a knowledge of the city. 'Shortcuts' and 'traffic light sets' affect his route choices. In Elias's narrative, his job as a deliverer is not shaped by the algorithmic distribution of orders, but by crafting a bike messenger identity.

IT MIGHT BE AN ILLUSION, BUT IT IS THERE

In the debate on platform food-delivery, there is a strong consensus that the business models investigated reduce workers to an adjunct of automated processes (Goods, Veen and Barratt 2019). Delivery workers become an intermediary element of the algorithm where the 'experience of a routine activity becomes near-automatic' (Waters and Woodcock 2017: 14). GPS-tracking produces constant time/motion studies, creates detailed performance control (Gandini 2018) and develops the quantification of human labour (Moore 2018). This line of research connects with social-philosophical ideas on machinic subordination, where human bodies are reduced to serve a larger productive mechanism (Deleuze and Guattari 2005; Lazzarato 2014). However, the literature on bicycle messengers highlights the autonomy that comes with navigating the city, which impacts how workers experience their shift (Kidder 2009; Fincham 2006).

The argument of this chapter is that the 'illusion of freedom' (Waters and Woodcock 2017) in these settings should be taken seriously. This is because organising workers in an attempt to increase bargaining power starts with workers, and in particular with how they perceive their work and the technology applied in their jobs.

The data shows that the production process relies on particular social relations, such as the workers subordinating to the algorithm. This was apparent, for instance, in the double order taken by Nick, but also in the narration of David, who misses the social relationships he was familiar with from other messenger services.

However, we have also seen that other aspects of the workday might hide these relations and thereby constitute a distinct experience of work (Jahoda 1982). We saw this in the story given by Tamino, who navigated in the most automated way but still enjoyed the work for its different aspects such as exploring new places. Elias also crafted an occupational identity that was untouched by the algorithmic dispatching of orders. Both reported about aspects of their work that were more important to them than how the algorithm assigns deliveries or how the company treats their data.

Several authors highlight the importance of taking workers' experiences seriously for social research (Moore 2018). This is especially relevant for research aiming to contribute to working-class power, as every struggle starts with the workers involved. The findings presented above indicate that algorithmic management might not be the most important force shaping workers' experience. While algorithms subordinate workers, the workers themselves might not feel this way. This suggests that criticising the algorithm may not be the most successful road. Workers' 'illusion of freedom' should be taken seriously, because gaining working-class power builds on people's experience and activities. It needs to depart from their very perception of their work, without affirming 'false consciousness'. It actually needs people to 'break' the algorithmic workplace.

REFERENCES

Burawoy, M. (1979). *Manufacturing Consent*. Chicago: University of Chicago Press.

Burawoy, M. (1985). *The Politics of Production*. London: Verso.

Deleuze, G. and Guattari, F. (2005). *A Thousand Plateaus: Capitalism and Schizophrenia*. Minneapolis: University of Minnesota.

Edwards, P. (1986). *Conflict at Work*. Oxford: Blackwell.

Fincham, B. (2006). Bicycle Messengers and the Road to Freedom. *The Sociological Review* 54(1), supplement, 208–22.

Friedman, A. (1977). Responsible Autonomy Versus Direct Control Over the Labour Process. *Capital & Class* 1(1), 43–57.

Gandini, A. (2018). Labour Process Theory and the Gig Economy. *Human Relations* 72(6), 1039–56.

Goods, C., Veen, A. and Barratt, T. (2019). 'Is Your Gig Any Good?' Analysing Job Quality in the Australian Platform-Based Food-Delivery Sector. *Journal of Industrial Relations*. At https://doi.org/10.1177/0022185618817069.

Griesbach, K., Reich, A., Elliott-Negri, L. and Milkman, R. (2019). Algorithmic Control in Platform Food Delivery Work. *Socius: Sociological Research for a Dynamic World* 5, 1–15.

Herr, B. (2017). Riding in the Gig Economy: An In-Depth Study of a Branch in the App-Based on-Demand Food Delivery Industry. Working Paper No. 169, Chamber of Labour, Vienna. At www.arbeiterkammer.at/infopool/wien/AK_Working_Paper_Riding_in_the_Gig_Economy.pdf.

Herr, B. (2018). *Ausgeliefert. Fahrräder, Apps Und Die Neue Art Der Essenzustellung.* Vienna: ÖGB Verlag.

Horkheimer, M. and Adorno, T. W. (2006). *Dialektik Der Aufklärung. Philosophische Fragmente.* Frankfurt am Main: Fischer Taschenbuchverlag.

Jahoda, M. (1982) *Employment and Unemployment: A Social-Psychological Analysis.* Cambridge: Cambridge University Press.

Jaros, S. J. (2005). Marxian Critiques of Thompson's (1990) 'Core' Labour Process Theory: An Evaluation and Extension. *Ephemera: Theory and Politics in Organization* 5(1), 5–25.

Kidder, J. L. (2009). Appropriating the City: Space, Theory, and Bike Messengers. *Theory and Society* 38(3), 307–28.

Lazzarato, M. (2014). *Signs and Machines: Capitalism and the Production of Subjectivity.* Los Angeles: semiotext(e).

Marx, K. (1962). *Das Kapital.* Dietz, Berlin: Der Produktionsprozeß Des Kapitals.

Moore, P. (2018). *The Quantified Self in Precarity: Work, Technology and What Counts.* London and New York: Routledge.

Shapiro, A. (2018). Between Autonomy and Control: Strategies of Arbitrage in the 'On-Demand' Economy. *New Media & Society* 20(8), 2954–71.

Srnicek, N. (2017). *Platform Capitalism.* Cambridge: Polity.

Tilly, C. and Tilly, C. (1998). *Work under Capitalism.* Boulder: Westview Press.

Veen, A., Barratt, T. and Goods, C. (2019). Platform-Capital's 'App-etite' for Control: A Labour Process Analysis of Food-Delivery Work in Australia. *Work, Employment and Society* 34(3), 388–406.

Waters, F. and Woodcock, J. (2017). Far from Seamless: A Workers' Inquiry at Deliveroo. *Viewpoint Magazine.* At www.viewpointmag.com/2017/09/20/far-seamless-workers-inquiry-deliveroo.

Woodcock, J. (2020). The Algorithmic Panopticon at Deliveroo: Measurement, Precarity, and the Illusion of Control. *Ephemera: Theory and Politics in Organization.* At www.ephemerajournal.org/contribution/algorithmic-panopticon-deliveroo-measurement-precarity-and-illusion-control.

4
Putting the Habitus to Work: Digital Prosumption, Surveillance and Distinction

Eduard Müller

THE DEVELOPMENT OF THEORIES OF PROSUMPTION

The insight that individual production and consumption can overlap and that a 'pure' dichotomy of the two processes lacks analytical accuracy goes back to the early stages of industrialisation and theorists like Karl Marx (Ritzer, Dean and Jurgenson 2012: 381).

When Alvin Toffler introduced the term 'prosumer' in his 1980 book *The Third Wave*, as a portmanteau of the words *producer* and *consumer*, he used it to describe his vision of consumers who would become increasingly integrated into the production phase itself, just as workers had been in pre-industrial societies. In his opinion, the dawning 'age of prosumption' would originate in a new participatory form of democracy, labour autonomy and self-determination. Although Toffler neglected to think about the possible negative outcomes of prosumption (Fuchs 2011: 297), his theoretical overcoming of the established manager-worker dyad in the field of organisation studies (Gabriel, Korczynski and Rieder 2015) represented a significant development.

A more differentiated prospect was delivered by George Ritzer (1993, 1999), who, similar to Toffler, saw societies entering a new stage of 'prosumer capitalism'. Ritzer argued that, even though prosumption has always been a part of socio-economic behaviour throughout human history, it would increasingly supersede consumer-centred capitalism in modern societies. In contrast to Toffler's euphoric vision, Ritzer also pointed out negative aspects of 'prosumer capitalism', for example 'new forms of economic exploitation, social injustice, and cultural alienation' (Zwick 2015: 485).

While these two early scholars predicted prosumers to be at the very heart of a new economic era, contemporary organisation studies did not pay substantial attention to their conceptualisations. This changed at the beginning of the twenty-first century, when business scholars began to adopt the theorisations on prosumption. Terms like 'co-opting' and 'value co-creation' (Prahalad and Ramaswamy 2000, 2002) emphasised a positive, business-friendly view of customers playing a bigger role in the production process. Another euphoric embrace came from Tapscott and Williams (2006: 15), who, similarly to Toffler and Ritzer, defined prosumption as the 'core activity' of a new economic system, which they envisioned as innovative, creative and leading to a 'new economic democracy'. During the mid- and late 2000s, when the term 'sharing economy' dominated the discourse on digitalisation as a positive notion, several other buzzwords and neologisms for prosumptive practices were created, such as 'user-generated content', 'crowdsourcing', 'user innovation', 'user participation', 'open source', 'playbour' or 'produser'.

Another substantial contribution to the theories on prosumption is Kerstin Rieder and Günter Voss's (2013) concept of the 'working customer'. Originally conceived in the mid-2000s, this theorisation was developed further over the following decade. According to its authors the conception of the 'working customer' has its origin in Voss and Pongratz's (1998) theoretical construct of the 'Arbeitskraftunternehmer' (i.e. workforce entrepreneur). Both ideas, the 'working customer' and the 'workforce entrepreneur', consider established relationships in the production processes of goods and services to be undergoing fundamental changes. Consequently, the 'workforce entrepreneur' is exerting enhanced self-control, efficiency-oriented self-exploitation, and self-management. The concept of the 'working customer' complements and expands this theorisation of delimitation. The three central characteristics that, according to Rieder and Voss (2013), define 'working customers' are as follows:

1. their status as a 'quasi-employee' (Rieder and Voss 2013: 4) in the production process;
2. they usually remain unpaid, even 'if customers provide services they don't use themselves, but that create added value ... for the enterprises' (Rieder and Voss 2013: 4);

3. they become employees, because they use means of production of corporations (e.g. software, vending machines, etc.) and the 'productive elements of individual consumption are subject to organisational rules and restrictions. However, these differ from people in gainful employment, in that their work has no official legal form, no legal protection and no lobby' (Rieder and Voss 2013: 5).

As a consequence, Rieder and Voss (2013) assume that the boundaries between the spheres of work and private life are undergoing a process of 'dual delimitation'. The 'workforce entrepreneurs' see their private resources and lives undercut by the employment process, while the 'working customers' see their private resources and lives usurped by unpaid work. While work outside established employment relations is nothing new, 'the current linkage of work for enterprises with the private lives of individuals is, however, completely new ... Accordingly, it makes sense to speak of a current erosion of private life which, until now, characterized society' (Rieder and Voss 2013: 7).

From a strand of critical media studies, Christian Fuchs (2010, 2011, 2014) revisited the concept of 'audience labour' (Smythe 1981) and applied Marxian theory to contemporary 'data capitalism' (West 2017). Fuchs notes that, in contrast to the earlier notion of 'audience labour', internet users are more active than the viewers of TV shows or readers of printed newspapers, because 'they engage in permanent creative activity, communication, community building, and content production'. Thus, the data produced by users during their online activity is being sold to advertising companies as an audience commodity. Fuchs concludes: 'Due to the permanent activity of the recipients and their status as prosumers, we can say that, in the case of the Internet, the audience commodity is a prosumer commodity' (2011: 298). As users generate data for corporations during most of their time spent online, Fuchs does not observe 'a democratization of the media towards a participatory or democratic system but rather the total commodification of human creativity' (2011: 301).

THE CONCEPTS OF DATA AND SURVEILLANCE CAPITALISM

The economic practice of extensive storage and brokerage of user data by corporations has been referred to as 'data capitalism' (West 2017) or 'surveillance capitalism' (Zuboff 2015). Media and scientific attention on this issue has risen since the revelations by former CIA agent Edward Snowden on the surveillance practices of the US-based telecommunication enterprises and the National Security Agency (NSA) in 2013 (West 2017: 4; Zuboff 2015: 86), and, more recently, with the scandal over the British consulting company Cambridge Analytica, which harvested the data of approximately 87 million Facebook users and employed it – without their consent – for advertising purposes in political campaigns in the US and other countries (Rosenberg, Confessore and Cadwalladr 2018). Furthermore, several multinational companies like Facebook or the online dating app Tinder (Duportail 2017), but also smaller companies like the Austrian public mail service, have been mining and selling data about their users.

With her concept of 'data capitalism' Sarah Myers West aims 'to describe consequences of the turn from an e-commerce model premised on the sale of goods online to an advertising model premised on the sale of audiences – or, more accurately, on the sale of individual behavioural profiles tied to user data' (2017: 4). Central to West's considerations are the tremendous information asymmetries between users and corporations, as the ability to harvest, analyse and commercialise digital traces is only available to a minority (2017: 18).

Similarly, media sociologist Shoshana Zuboff observes a structure of informational and juridical asymmetries between users and big technology corporations like Google or Facebook. She postulates a 'fully institutionalized new logic of accumulation that I have called surveillance capitalism ... In this new regime, a global architecture of computer mediation turns the electronic text of the bounded organization into an intelligent world-spanning organism that I call Big Other' (2015: 85). Zuboff refers to Karl Polanyi's (1957) concept of fictious (or fake) commodities, which describes the treatment of nature, labour and human beings as mere commodities. With regard to the economic practices of data capitalism, she deduces that this form of capitalising on newly perceived business opportunities challenges social norms concerning privacy and is therefore socially contested as a juridical violation.

Summarising this selective overview of theories on prosumption and data capitalism, four major conclusions can be drawn:

1. While the various theorisations of prosumption clearly differ in their critical approach, most of them argue that, by means of technological progress, customers will become an integral part of corporate business models.
2. Due to their rising embeddedness in the creation of profits through increasing digitalisation, 'digital prosumers' likewise become more integrated in organisations offering goods and services than previous forms of prosumers.
3. 'Working customers' or 'prosumers', even though they might receive rebates or other incentives during the production process, provide unpaid labour or unpaid information.
4. While several ambiguities of 'digital prosumption' and data capitalism have been stressed by the main theories listed above, most of them lack a more comprehensive approach to the different sorts of capital of the prosumers which are being employed, harvested and sold. This might result from a Marxian definition of capital, as it has been applied by some scholars (Comor 2015; Fuchs 2011; Ritzer and Jurgenson 2010). Consequently, the Bourdieusian theorisations on multiple forms of capital, social fields and habitus will be elucidated and subsequently integrated.

DIGITAL PROSUMERS, ORGANISATIONS AND BOURDIEU'S RELATIONAL SOCIOLOGY

While the relational sociology of French scholar Pierre Bourdieu has received increasing attention in organisation studies since the 1980s, its integration remained mostly fragmented and indirect (Hallett and Gougherty 2018: 273f). Though the Bourdieusian concepts of social fields and capital (Bourdieu 1989, 2008) have been employed in organisational research, Emirbayer and Johnson argue that 'the third concept in Bourdieu's triad – habitus – has been applied to the study of organisations only a handful of times' (2008: 4). This section will give an appropriately brief definition of these main Bourdieusian concepts and then apply them to the strand of recent prosumption theorisations.

Social fields

In Bourdieu's view, social life occurs in fields that are arenas of struggle. In those fields, participants take positions relative to each other and share a common understanding of 'the socially constructed, centralised framework of meaning, or what is at stake in the field. Bourdieu's fields are relatively autonomous, meaning each tends to have its own logic (or "rules of the game") and history' (Kluttz and Fligstein 2016: 189). Sticking with Bourdieu's game metaphor, players, i.e. social actors, compete with each other for positions, status and especially for the power to define the 'rules of the game' which dominate the social relations in the field. Additionally, multiple social fields may overlap or influence each other, as many sub-fields are embedded in wider social contexts and dependencies. In Bourdieu's conceptualisation, dominating individuals or groups exert power over others by using their ability to control what is at stake (Kluttz and Fligstein 2016: 189). This domination tends to take 'disguised forms' the more resistance grows and if continuation of existing power imbalances becomes more difficult (Bourdieu 1990: 128).

Capital

The main source of dominance in social fields is the capital that individuals and groups contribute to the field. Bourdieu (2008: 16f) identifies three fundamental forms of capital, namely economic, social and cultural capital. He conceptualises the latter also as 'symbolic capital', because its conditions of appropriation and circulation are more disguised than those of economic capital. Therefore, Bourdieu considers cultural capital 'predisposed to function as symbolic capital, i.e., to be unrecognised as capital and recognised as legitimate competence, as authority exerting an effect of (mis) recognition' (2008: 18). Basically, the varying forms of capital are convertible into one another, but the conditions, quality and costs of this transformation can vary at given times (Emirbayer and Johnson 2008: 11). Consequently, social actors reproduce and contest power relations in fields based on their capital endowments (Kluttz and Fligstein 2016: 189). With his theorisation of capital, Bourdieu decisively expands the Marxian definition of capital and thus also our understanding of the effect of capital on the dynamics of social persistence and change.

Habitus

The third major concept in Bourdieusian field theory is his definition of 'habitus' (Bourdieu 2010). Habitus, internalised via socialisation, is the 'bundle of cognitive and evaluative capacities that make up one's perceptions, judgments, tastes, and strategies for actions' (Kluttz and Fligstein 2016: 189). The strategies and actions taken by actors in social fields are generated by the habitus, as it 'enables actors to apprehend, navigate, and act in the social world' (Kluttz and Fligstein 2016: 189). Bourdieu argues that the social modes of producing habitus are 'an integral part of the conditions of reproduction of the social order and of the productive apparatus itself, which could not function without the dispositions that the group inculcates' (1990: 130). The habitus itself is a result of the social structures and order it tends to reproduce (Bourdieu 1990: 160). It is simultaneously a system of production of practices as well as a system of perceiving and appreciating practices (Bourdieu 1989).

Despite the central role it has in Bourdieu's theoretical framework, the concept of the habitus has been widely neglected within organisational research. As Emirbayer and Johnson emphasise, this 'almost total inattention to habitus, ... without which the concepts of field and capital ... make no sense, further attests to the misappropriation of [Bourdieu's] ideas and to the lack of appreciation of their potential usefulness' (2008: 2).

Field theory and prosumption

In relation to the social phenomenon of (digital) prosumption, all three major concepts of Bourdieusian field theory can reveal enriching insights for both organisation studies and field theory. Following Hallett and Gougherty's suggestion, it seems advisable to 'expand Bourdieu's relational sociology by considering organizational interactions as social relations, pregnant with symbolic power and possible conflict; shaped by habitus, cultural capital, and the institutional landscape, but not completely determined by them, and not inconsequential for understanding organizational life' (Hallett and Gougherty 2018: 288). Lisa Suckert (2017: 427) points out that a Bourdieusian field theoretical approach can be especially enriching for present economic sociology, because it emphasises obscured power relations and contestations as well as historical aspects of economic coordination. As Tim Hallett notes: 'In completing organizational tasks, people act on the basis not only of formal organisational rules, but also of the habitus' (2003: 130).

One task that has become ubiquitous in the course of expanding digitalisation is the evaluation of services and goods by users. In most cases this may be done in the form of multi-scale scores and/or comments (Kornberger, Pflueger and Mouritsen 2017; Rosenblat and Stark 2016). These rating systems reduce insecurity about transactions in social interactions. In the production of services and goods they are therefore applied to minimise the 'transformation problem' (Braverman 1974), i.e. the transformation from capacity to work to actually rendered work performance at the highest possible surplus value. On the basis of Bourdieu's concepts of capital, Marion Fourcade and Francis Healy developed their concept of 'übercapital' to grasp the position takings and leeway in the digital social space: 'Übercapital overlaps with the traditional forms identified by Bourdieu but also departs from them. It has a clear materiality, and a numerical form ... It is subject to calculation ... Its materiality makes übercapital a contingent empirical phenomenon ... We can think of übercapital as made up of all the digital information available about an individual' (Fourcade and Healy 2017: 10). Thus, the personnel in platform-mediated service industries are in competition for positive user evaluations in order to build a successful digital reputation. Vice versa, in some cases the customers themselves become subject to evaluations by the workforce.

The deployment of online rankings is increasing in sectors like hospitality brokerage (e.g. Airbnb, booking.com), taxi services (Uber, Lyft) and e-commerce (eBay, Amazon). Since control over the specific design of the rating systems remains on the side of the platforms, users are only able (and permitted) to evaluate a few aspects of the services they consume. As Tom Slee observes, 'We are left with a relatively narrow range of trust problems that reputation systems can even claim to address: cleanliness, punctuality, friendliness and so on' (2017: 93). The perception of a sufficiently friendly waiter, a properly tidied room or an aggressive driver is, from a Bourdieusian perspective, a question of taste and preference and is therefore deeply connected with the habitus. Acknowledging the concept of habitus as being distinctive for more complex dispositions – for example individual or collective preference systems and economic attitudes (Suckert 2017: 418) – opens up an enriching sociological perspective on these new forms of evaluative practices. Moreover, the rating practices applied in service sectors can increase the risks of discrimination, physical and psychosocial violence and harassment (Moore, Akhtar and Upchurch 2018), as research on taxi (Rosenblat et al. 2017) and hospitality (Edelman and Luca 2014) platforms indicates. From a Bourdieusian standpoint, this represents the reproduction of existing social inequalities and has to be addressed by the organisations that apply these digital management methods.

CONCLUSIONS

This chapter set out to emphasise the importance of a thorough integration of Bourdieusian field theory in organisation studies for a better understanding of the fundamentally transformed role of prosumers in platform capitalism. 'Working customers' carry out managerial tasks, and highly personal information on their online and offline behaviour is being commercialised, in many cases illicitly, by platform organisations. While the theorisations of the French philosopher and sociologist Michel Foucault on power, organisations and control increasingly receive attention from scholars researching digitalisation (Fuchs 2011; Kirchner and Schüssler 2019; Kornberger, Pflueger and Mouritsen 2017), Bourdieu's concepts remain scarcely implemented in this field of research (Cole 2011). Similarly, the present labour processes involving digital prosumption are mainly discussed from Marxian perspectives on capital, alienation and exploitation.

Fully applying the Bourdieusian concepts of field and habitus (Bourdieu 2010; Hillebrandt 2017) in the research strand of prosumption and organisations can help us understand a wide variety of questions and problems arising from the phenomenon of 'digital prosumption'. In particular, the idea of the customer's habitus, which is being increasingly integrated in organisational relations via the rising number of digital prosumptive practices (Antonio 2015), has a high explanatory power. The commodification of users' behaviour, of their social ties and their political, cultural and other preferences, effectively appears like an attempt to commodify the users' very habitus itself. The cases in which big centralised corporations observe users and subsequently decide which political or cultural information they should receive represent instances of social exclusion and the reproduction of social imbalances. As a consequence, civil rights and data protection regulations are contested in most markets involving platform organisations, and the public demand for more transparency in the platforms' use of collected user data is growing (Flyverbom et al. 2016; Galloway 2011). Consulting Bourdieusian field theory can also advance our understanding of these struggles and contestations, as the elucidation of power imbalances and social conflicts is one of the major strengths of this theory strand.

REFERENCES

Antonio, R. J. (2015). Is Prosumer Capitalism on the Rise? *The Sociological Quarterly* 56, 472–83.

Bourdieu, P. (1989). Social Space and Symbolic Power. *Sociological Theory* 7, 14–25.

Bourdieu, P. (1990). *The Logic of Practice*. Stanford: Stanford University Press.

Bourdieu, P. (2008). The Forms of Capital. In N. W. Biggart, ed. *Readings in Economic Sociology*. Hoboken: John Wiley & Sons, 280–91.

Bourdieu, P. (2010). *Distinction*. London: Routledge.

Braverman, H. (1974). *Labor and Monopoly Capital: The Degradation of Work in the Twentieth Century*. New York: Monthly Review Press.

Cole, S. J. (2011). The Prosumer and the Project Studio: The Battle for Distinction in the Field of Music Recording. *Sociology* 45. At https://doi.org/10.1177/0038038511399627.

Comor, E. (2015). Revisiting Marx's Value Theory: A Critical Response to Analyses of Digital Prosumption. *The Information Society* 31, 13–19.

Duportail, J. (2017). I Asked Tinder For My Data. It Sent Me 800 Pages of My Deepest, Darkest Secrets. *Guardian*, 26 September. At www.theguardian.com/technology/2017/sep/26/tinder-personal-data-dating-app-messages-hacked-sold.

Edelman, B. G. and Luca, M. (2014). *Digital Discrimination: The Case of Airbnb.com*. SSRN Scholarly Paper Nr. ID 2377353. Rochester, NY: Social Science Research Network.

Emirbayer, M. and Johnson, V. (2008). Bourdieu and Organizational Analysis. *Theory and Society* 37(1), 1–44.

Flyverbom, M., Leonardi, P., Stohl, C. and Stohl, M. (2016). The Management of Visibilities in the Digital Age: Introduction. *International Journal of Communication* 10, 98–109.

Fourcade, M. and Healy, K. (2017). Seeing Like a Market. *Socio-Economic Review* 15, 9–29.

Fuchs, C. (2010). Labor in Informational Capitalism and on the Internet. *The Information Society* 26, 179–96.

Fuchs, C. (2011). Web 2.0, Prosumption, and Surveillance. *Surveillance & Society* 8, 288–309.

Fuchs, C. (2014). Digital Prosumption Labour on Social Media in the Context of the Capitalist Regime of Time. *Time & Society* 23, 97–123.

Gabriel, Y., Korczynski, M. and Rieder, K. (2015). Organizations and Their Consumers: Bridging Work and Consumption. *Organization* 22, 629–43.

Galloway, A. (2011). Black Box, Black Bloc. In B. Noys, ed. *Communization and Its Discontents: Contestation, Critique, and Contemporary Struggles*. New York: Minor Compositions, 237–49.

Hallett, T. (2003). Symbolic Power and Organizational Culture. *Sociological Theory* 21, 128–49.

Hallett, T. and Gougherty, M. (2018). Bourdieu and Organizations. In T. Medvetz and J. J. Sallaz, eds. *The Oxford Handbook of Pierre Bourdieu*. Oxford: Oxford University Press, 273–98.

Hillebrandt, F. (2017). Pierre Bourdieu: The Social Structure of the Economy. In K. Kraemer and F. Brugger, eds. *Schlüsselwerke der Wirtschaftssoziologie*. Wiesbaden: Springer VS, 343–9.

Kirchner, S. and Schüssler, E. (2019). The Organization of Digital Marketplaces: Unmasking the Role of Internet Platforms in the Sharing Economy. In G. Ahrne and N. Brunsson, eds. *Organization outside Organizations. The Abundance of Partial Organization in Social Life*. Cambridge: Cambridge University Press, 131–54.

Kluttz, D. N. and Fligstein, N. (2016). Varieties of Sociological Field Theory. In S. Abrutyn, ed. *Handbook of Contemporary Sociological Theory*. New York: Springer International, 185–204.

Kornberger, M., Pflueger, D. and Mouritsen, J. (2017). Evaluative Infrastructures: Accounting for Platform Organization. *Accounting, Organizations and Society* 60, 79–95.

Moore, P. V., Akhtar, P. and Upchurch, M. (2018). Digitalisation of Work and Resistance. In P. V. Moore, M. Upchurch and X. Whittaker, eds. *Humans and Machines at Work: Monitoring, Surveillance and Automation in Contemporary Capitalism*. Cham: Springer International, 17–44.

Polanyi, K. (1957). *The Great Transformation*. Boston: Beacon Press.

Prahalad, C. K. and Ramaswamy, V. (2000). Co-opting Customer Competence. *Harvard Business Review* (January–February). At https://hbr.org/2000/01/co-opting-customer-competence.

Prahalad, C. K. and Ramaswamy, V. (2002). The Co-Creation Connection. *Strategy & Business* 27, 51–60.

Rieder, K. and Voss, G. G. (2013). The Working Customer: A Fundamental Change in Service Work. In W. Dunkel and F. Kleemann, eds. *Customers at Work: New Perspectives on Interactive Service Work*. Basingstoke: Palgrave Macmillan, 177–96.

Ritzer, G. (1993). *The McDonaldization of Society: An Investigation Into the Changing Character of Contemporary Social Life*. Newbury Park: Pine Forge Press.

Ritzer, G. (1999). *Enchanting a Disenchanted World: Revolutionizing the Means of Consumption*. Newbury Park: Pine Forge Press.

Ritzer, G. and Jurgenson, N. (2010). Production, Consumption, Prosumption: The Nature of Capitalism in the Age of the Digital 'Prosumer'. *Journal of Consumer Culture* 10, 13–36.

Ritzer, G., Dean, P. and Jurgenson, N. (2012). The Coming of Age of the Prosumer. *American Behavioral Scientist* 56, 379–98.

Rosenberg, M., Confessore, N. and Cadwalladr, C. (2018). How Trump Consultants Exploited the Facebook Data of Millions. *New York Times*, 17 March. At www.nytimes.com/2018/03/17/us/politics/cambridge-analytica-trump-campaign.html.

Rosenblat, A. and Stark, L. (2016). Algorithmic Labor and Information Asymmetries: A Case Study of Uber's Drivers. *International Journal of Communication* 10, 3758–84.

Rosenblat, A., Levy, K. E. C., Barocas, S. and Hwang, T. (2017). Discriminating Tastes: Uber's Customer Ratings as Vehicles for Workplace Discrimination. *Policy & Internet* 9, 256–79.

Slee, T. (2017). *What's Yours Is Mine: Against the Sharing Economy*. New York: OR Books.

Smythe, D. W. (1981). On the Audience Commodity and its Work. In M. G. Durham and D. M. Kellner, eds. *Media and Cultural Studies: KeyWorks*. Oxford: Blackwell, 230–56.

Suckert, L. (2017). Same Same But Different. Die Feldtheorien Fligsteins und Bourdieus und das Potenzial einer wechselseitig informierten Perspektive für die Wirtschaftssoziologie. *Berliner Journal für Soziologie* 27, 405–30.

Tapscott, D. and Williams, A. D. (2006). *Wikinomics: How Mass Collaboration Changes Everything*. New York: Portfolio.

Tucker, C. (2019). Privacy, Algorithms, and Artificial intelligence. In Agarwal, A. Gans, J. and Goldfarb, A. (eds.). *The Economics of Artificial Intelligence: An Agenda*. National Bureau of Economic Research. Chicago and London: The University of Chicago Press, 423–38.

Voss, G. and Pongratz, H. (1998). Der Arbeitskraftunternehmer: Eine Neue Grundform der Ware Arbeitskraft? *Kölner Zeitschrift für Soziologie und Sozialpsychologie* 50(1), 131–58.

Voss, G. and Rieder, K. (2005). *Der arbeitende Kunde: Wenn Konsumenten zu unbezahlten Mitarbeitern werden*. Frankfurt am Main: Campus Verlag.

West, S. M. (2017). Data Capitalism: Redefining the Logics of Surveillance and Privacy. *Business & Society*. At https://doi.org/10.1177/0007650317718185.

Zuboff, S. (2015). Big Other: Surveillance Capitalism and the Prospects of an Information Civilization. *Journal of Information Technology* 30, 75–89.

Zwick, D. (2015). Defending the Right Lines of Division: Ritzer's Prosumer Capitalism in the Age of Commercial Customer Surveillance and Big Data. *The Sociological Quarterly* 56, 484–98.

5
The Power of Prediction: People Analytics at Work

Uwe Vormbusch and Peter Kels

By collecting and connecting huge amounts of data, people analytics not only promises to raise the effectiveness of people management practices (Manuti and de Palma 2018; Goodell King 2016; Sullivan 2013) but to establish new possibilities to evaluate and control staff. From the perspective of 'knowledge capitalism', people analytics is but one relevant field in which actors strive 'to make the intangible assets employees ... embody computable and calculable' (Vormbusch 2007: 92) – an intimately linked one is the invention of 'taxonomies of the self' (Moore and Robinson 2016; Vormbusch 2020). Consequently, in his analysis of the legal implications of predictive policing in the US, Ferguson states that there is a veritable array of 'future predictive techniques' (2017: 1115). From this overarching perspective, data-driven strategies such as predictive policing, predictive HR and recommendation systems for music and accommodation are equally striving for 'controlling the future' (Vormbusch 2009). These systems intend to shape future behaviour as well as the political, cultural and normative frames within which future action is going to happen. They represent separate modules of a governmentality of the future not yet connected and not yet accomplished. In the case of people analytics, the entire communication of workers – their emails, their daily use of phone and social media, their occupational and even private networks – are to be scanned then merged in a unified data space, allowing Human Resources and an emerging rank of data specialists to create 'data doubles' (Haggerty and Ericson 2000) readily available for manifold analysis.

In a *first step*, we will outline the general concept of people analytics with special attention to management expectations and definitions, areas of application and the specific knowledge produced by these systems, drawing on management literature. In a *second step*, we will illustrate typical practices of algorithmic observation, stimulation and prediction of employees' work, learning and performance. In a *final step*, we will discuss the implications of predictive analytics for control and co-determination, participation and subjectivity.

PEOPLE ANALYTICS: DEFINITIONS, MANAGEMENT EXPECTATIONS, AREAS OF APPLICATION

People analytics (synonyms: workforce analytics, HR analytics) can be defined as an 'HR practice enabled by information technology that uses descriptive, visual, and statistical analyses of data related to HR processes, human capital, organizational performance, and external economic benchmarks to establish business impact and enable data-driven decision-making' (Marler and Boudreau 2017: 15). People analytics allow algorithm-based and thus automated screening, analysis and processing of extensive personal and personnel-related data and behavioural traces, based on:

1. Information about employees collected in personnel information systems, such as performance and competence assessments, certificates, applications, etc.
2. Publicly accessible information about applicants or employees and their social network (e.g. Xing, LinkedIn or Facebook).
3. All conceivable traces of behaviour such as the communication and work behaviour of employees and their occupational networking, which can be recorded and merged via location data from online collaboration tools, office applications, intranet or emails (cf. Deloitte 2018; Höller and Wedde 2018; Strohmeier 2017; Angrave et al. 2016; Christ and Ebert 2016).

Potential areas of application include the entire value chain of human resources management. Based on the insights gained, 'employee recognition programs, enterprise learning, onboarding, resource planning, HR reporting, competency management, talent acquisition, learning and development, succession management [or] reward' may be optimised (Sousa et al. 2019: 6; also cf. Mishra, Raghvendra Lama and Pal 2016; Goodell King 2016; Khan and Tang 2017).

People analytics is part of a postulated management revolution, in which people and performance-related data are brought together as the basis for data-driven decision-making (Davenport 2006). In this sense, Google, Procter & Gamble and other innovating companies 'have taken the guesswork out of employee management' (Davenport, Harris and Shapiro 2010: 1). Since such an 'evidence-based' form of management is presumed to be decisive for competitive advantages, the growing interest of HR practitioners, consultancy firms and software development companies in people analytics comes as no surprise. *First*, with the increasing complexity and digitisation of work processes, companies are becoming more and more interested in the data-based recording, monitoring, control and optimisation of work activities and the performance potential of their employees. *Second*, HR departments traditionally have difficulties meeting expectations in terms of measuring how and which HR practices contribute to corporate goals or value creation (Brüggemann and Schinnenburg 2018). While many other departments like finance or marketing have established data-based accountability and control systems, the '"talent" information infrastructure remains quite underdeveloped in most companies, at least in proportion to its expected value' (Huselid 2018: 680). As it has now become possible to use smart applications to capture and analyse comprehensive personal and behavioural data in real time in the cloud, people analytics are perceived as a powerful tool for revolutionising the HR function and raising its effectiveness (Manuti and de Palma 2018: 40). As Angrave and colleagues state, one key question is how 'existing, essentially descriptive HR analytics programmes (can) evolve to focus on measuring and modelling the strategic impact of human capital inputs so creating better management decision tools' (Angrave et al. 2016: 6).

PREDICTIVE PEOPLE ANALYTICS AT WORK

Advanced Predictive People Analytics (PPA) go far beyond traditional 'Descriptive Analytics' which use retrospective metrics (e.g. fluctuation rates or recruitment). With the aid of data mining, machine learning and advanced statistical methods, PPA are designed to monitor and track work behaviours of individuals and groups, analyse people data to identify relationships not readily explored, and build models in order to predict the future behaviour of individuals or groups (Mishra et al. 2016; Christ and

Ebert 2016; Goodell King 2016; Holthaus, Park and Stock-Homburg 2015). 'Measuring employee performance and engagement, studying workforce collaboration patterns, analysing employee churn and turnover and modelling employee lifetime value' thus form a basis for strategic and operational management decisions (Mishra et al. 2016: 33).

While the prescriptive management literature emphasises the new depths of insight 'into employees' personal and professional lives' and their 'attitude, behavior, personality, and aptitude' (Jain and Maitri 2018: 201) in order to optimise HR and performance management processes, empirical studies on the implementation of PPA and its consequences for HR decision-making and the labour process are largely missing. Nevertheless, Madsen and Slåtten (2017) analyse the rise of HR analytics from the perspective of 'Management Fashion Theory', and McDonald, Thompson and O'Connor (2016) scrutinise the 'profiling' of employees. Within the relatively narrow field of existing literature, lack of skilled personnel and competences in HR departments, as well as data integration and labour and data protection issues, are mentioned as explanations for obstacles to implementation (Minbaeva 2018; Brüggemann and Schinnenburg 2018; Angrave et al. 2016), indicating that so far probably only some pioneering companies have gained experience with predictive analytics tools.

Based on the examples of IBM's Watson Analytics and Microsoft Delve described by Gherson (2018) and Höller and Wedde (2018), we will briefly illustrate two major PPA applications. Diane Gherson, HR Senior Vice President at IBM, states:

> Using Watson Analytics, we can use the digital footprint within the company to draw conclusions about an employee's level of knowledge and compare it with the level he or she should have reached within his or her particular occupational group. The system works cognitively, it knows you. It has collected the data about your skills and can therefore make personal learning recommendations ... The system also checks what you are missing before the next digital award and suggests webinars and internal or external courses to you in order to obtain them ... All this is based on artificial intelligence. (Gherson 2018: 33)

Moreover, Watson Analytics is able to monitor sentiments and predict mood changes within the workforce based on the electronic communication of employees. The underlying goal of this real-time monitoring practice, proclaimed by Gherson, is to provide a highly agile early warning system that can detect problems and sources of conflict before they become virulent:

> Mood analyses are always helpful in a world where people are constantly commenting on everything online. Our cognitive technologies look at people's choice of words and pick up on pitch. They recognize whether it is positive or negative. All this happens exclusively behind our firewall, never externally ... With this approach, you'll quickly see if there's an area you need to look at. (Gherson 2018: 34–5)

Höller and Wedde (2018: 33ff.) describe how this preventive monitoring practice using Watson Analytics works. They concentrate on the possibilities for analysing employee performance, internal groups ('cliques') and their cooperative relationships, as well as the entire informal corporate network – its 'social graph'. The analysis of behavioural traces focuses on the so-called 'Engagement Analytics'. Here, a kind of cockpit ('Personal Social Dashboard') allows each employee to understand in an aggregated and clear form who is actually reading their email, who is reacting to them, who liked, forwarded or commented on their contributions in the company's social media platforms – and to adapt their behaviour accordingly. A 'total score' of the employee's commitment is algorithmically generated on an ongoing basis, consisting of the parameters 'activity', 'reaction', 'eminence' and 'network'. How these parameters are actually computed remains proprietary knowledge. Nevertheless, they are producing a very fine-grained picture of every individual's activities and 'worth' within the social graph. Accordingly, 'Engagement Analytics' are the ultimate tool for employees in a connectionist world (cf. Boltanski and Chiapello 2005) to comprehensively manage their organisational visibility, project competence and social reputation. It implies a new quality of subjectivising control and self-optimisation in the company with regard to their level of detail, their social reach and their penetration into the communicative environment of employees.

In the case of Watson as well as its Microsoft counterpart Delve (one of its Office 365 applications; see Swearingen 2015) the users – and presumably the human resource experts in the companies as well – are unaware of how the individual scores are calculated and condensed into an overall score. This remains proprietary knowledge well hidden from the individual customers.

Consequently, having no clue how to reconstruct the final result of the calculations permanently running in the informational background, neither the employees nor the works council will be able to renegotiate suggestions or decisions based on these calculations. Interestingly, IBM and Microsoft are no ordinary users here but service providers for thousands of different companies using their software and to whom they offer specifically tailored evaluations with regard to their respective 'social graphs'. IBM and Microsoft are thus in the exclusive position of accumulating enormous data, by means of which analyses can be carried out not only of dynamic changes in company moods, but also of mood swings and 'trendy' topics in entire industries. This allows for prediction on an entirely different level of industries or even entire economies, and might be invaluable for strategic investors within the financial markets wanting to know how the investment climate may be changing. Even if the validity and reliability of such knowledge is debatable, it is not unlikely to have performative effects, thereby making itself more 'true' in the process of being adopted (cf. MacKenzie and Millo 2003). Connecting social and corporate data brings a huge strategic advantage and is regarded as the rationale for Microsoft's acquisition of LinkedIn in 2016 and for Facebook entering the market for enterprise connectivity platforms with its 'Workplace' application the same year.

DISCUSSION

Obviously, PPA is focusing on the immaterial aspects of labour. It is not the first control system to do so (e.g., Team Work, specific incentive pay systems, management by objectives (MbO)), but it does so in an all-encompassing way. As an organisation technology, PPA draws heavily on the logic of social networks. Since it relies on data rather than bolts and joints (cf. the conveyor belt as the paradigmatic organisation technology during Taylor-Fordism), it could theoretically achieve an unsurpassed flexibility in the data-driven combination of ever more data (Big Data). This potential for creating novel insights by combining so far unrelated information about behavioural traces and people data is severely restricted by basic concepts inscribed into the sketched system. Core measures such as 'activity', 'reaction', 'prestige' and 'eminence' (built into IBM's 'Personal Social Dashboard' – Microsoft Delve uses a similar a similar technology, 'Delve Organisational Analytics') define the value of individual employees in the context of the organisational social graph, just like the evaluation algorithms used by Facebook and Instagram. By doing so they define a decontextualised, even rigid standard against which every single employee is measured. The measures of 'activity' and 'eminence' are by no means just mirroring what people are doing and valuing, rather they are standardising and prescribing what a 'valuable' employee is expected to do. They represent normative standards within the cognitive and evaluative framework of the latest management fashion. Since there is no commonly shared yardstick for immaterial labour or knowledge-based work (that is, measures for social ordering such as 'engagement', 'reputation', 'eminence' or 'social networking'), these systems actually invent new metrics derived from social network analysis. Employees are thereby positioned in a new kind of social and organisational hierarchy. Measuring and quantifying in this sense does not simply count what might be there before the counting, it is about 'creat[ing] new kinds and categories of things' (Espeland and Stevens 2008: 405). It brings forth the very categories in which people are supposed to think about themselves and are organisationally valued and gratified *without* regard to their concrete individuality. Since the categories of systems such as Delve and Watson are not just measuring how many standardised work packages an employee has completed, but rather social relations which are crucial for the identity and self-esteem of the individual, this neglect of the subjects' individuality is all the more severe. What does this imply?

First, the fact that every employee has his or her own ways of building networks, communicating with people and transforming data into meaning is completely neglected, making current PPA a system of social normalisation and coercion rather than just a collaborative work tool. Even though 'diversity' not only in public discourse but as a management mantra has gained so much attention lately, the construction of employees' worth within Delve and Watson is fundamentally ignoring this. Within this algorithmically constructed social performance culture a paradox is emerging: On the one hand, management theories about the future of organisation, work and the market are conceptualised as dynamic, volatile and open as never before. On the other hand, a substantial normalisation with respect to workers' desired attributes is inscribed into the system of predictive analytics, thereby not only harming individuals' diversity and individuality but also jeopardising the system's very objective of coping with volatile futures.

Second, concealing the underlying parameters for calculating core measures from those directly affected as well as the corporation's management and HR specialists has consequences on at least two levels: First, the managerial justification for being measured and valued in this particular way does not necessarily resonate with the evaluative concepts implicitly used by the workforce as well as the informal organisational culture, probably leading to discomfort, irritation or even resistance – most likely in the case of specialists and knowledge workers who are used to doing things their own way (including their own way of building social networks of trust and competence). And second, the 'rise of new forms of corporate power, based on the economic value of "data"' (Lodge and Mennicken 2017: 2) has legal implications not yet studied: Deliberately black-boxing how the communication patterns of thousands of employees are transformed into quantified data and into management decisions is rendering the entire system of corporate co-determination ineffective. In this context, Höller and Wedde (2018) point out that the big players within the emerging field of data politics not only have deep insights into the social graph of a single corporation but also command a broad as well as quite detailed knowledge of hundreds or even thousands of corporations in one industry or even across the boundaries of industries. A new layer of intercorporate control is thus emerging with tight oligopolies as nodes, overseeing the social graphs of single corporations, industries and even across industries. On the corporate level, a new class of data specialists is being constituted with the explicit task of monitoring and manipulating the social graph. Depending on their organisational affiliation, these knowledge workers command either corporate data or in some cases data provided and aggregated by some of the biggest and most powerful corporations on the globe, which are processing the data of thousands of corporations, then selling data-based analyses back to their clients. This emerging service class of data specialists represents a new centre of economic power. It will depend not only on the concrete division of labour between corporations such as IBM, Microsoft and even Facebook analysing data from above, and the average corporate customer just utilising their social graph, but also on which loyalties this service class will develop and how this will change the political balance within the corporation. Do algorithms and Big Data overturn the established lines of conflict in work organisations in the sense that the contested balance between workers and management is overlapped by an emerging conflict between a new class of data specialists on the one hand, and workers, HR managers and middle management on the other? Is algorithmic knowledge therefore unintendedly leading to shifting alliances on the shopfloor? In a predominantly prescriptive management literature neither the possible effects of such a monitoring culture on labour politics nor the fact that the employer has a special duty of care when collecting, storing, processing and evaluating personal data are sufficiently addressed. In this context, Brüggemann and Schinnenburg (2018) observe that predictive HR analytics are currently used more extensively by corporations in the Anglo-American and Asian regions than by companies in the EU, since labour and data protection laws are formulated much more freely there than within the framework of EU legislation.

Equally unclear is what opportunities workers under the regime of data-driven control still have to evade corporate control if every single *like* on corporate collaboration and social media platforms, every single email they are writing, is captured and algorithmically weighted, thereby extracting large quantities of unpaid 'data labour'. This implies a new quality of subjectivising control and self-optimisation with regard to the workers' entire social network and communicative behaviour. It might well be the employees with the best fit to the systems' inscribed normativities who will be capable of 'gaming the system'. In a continuation of control systems such as Team Work and MbO, PPA could easily be understood as a data-driven attempt to further commensurate the real heterogeneity of life. To be highly valued by these systems inevitably requires mobilising an even bigger share of one's social life and competencies as a means of competition (be it for promotion and a pay rise or just to stay in the game). This might further deepen the trenches between employees of different social competence and origin. MbO, HR portfolios, team work and incentive pay systems only partially succeeded in opening the treasure chest of living subjectivity. People analytics is a data-driven attempt to finally achieve this ambition by commensurating and quantifying workers' social life, transforming it into a 'social graph' up for sale.

REFERENCES

Angrave, D., Charlwood, A., Kirkpatrick, I., Lawrence, M. and Stuart, M. (2016). HR and Analytics: Why HR Is Set to Fail the Big Data Challenge. *Human Resource Management* 26(1), 1–11.

Biemann, T. and Weckmüller, H. (2016). Mensch gegen Maschine: Wie gut sind Algorithmen im HR? *Personal Quarterly* 68(4), 44–7.

Boltanski, L. and Chiapello, E. (2005). *The New Spirit of Capitalism*. London: Verso.

Brüggemann, C. and Schinnenburg, H. (2018). Predictive HR Analytics. Möglichkeiten und Grenzen des Einsatzes im Personalbereich. *ZfO* 87, 330–6.

Cachelin, J. L. (2013). Big Data Mining im HRM. Wie die Transparenz der Daten bessere Entscheidungen im HRM ermöglicht. Studie 6 der Wissensfabrik, September.

Christ, O. and Ebert, N. (2016). Predictive Analytics im Human Capital Management: Status Quo und Potentiale. *HMD* 53, 298–309.

Davenport, Th.H. (2006). Competing on Analytics. *Harvard Business Review*, January, 1–9.

Davenport, Th.H., Harris, J. and Shapiro, J. (2010). Competing on Talent Analytics. *Harvard Business Review*, October, 1–6.

Deloitte (2018). Global Human Capital Trends 2018: The Rise of the Social Enterprise. At www2.deloitte.com/insights/us/en/focus/human-capital-trends.html.

Espeland, W. and Stevens, M. (2008). A Sociology of Quantification. *European Journal of Sociology* 49(3), 401–36.

Ferguson, A. G. (2017). Policing Predictive Policing. *Washington University Law Review* 94(5), 1109–89.

Gherson, D. (2018). Glückliche Mitarbeiter, Glückliche Kunden. Interview in *Harvard Business Manager*, July, 32–5.

Goodell King, K. (2016). Data Analytics in Human Resources: A Case Study and Critical Review. *Human Resource Development Review* 15(4), 487–95.

Haggerty, K. D. and Ericson, R. V. (2000). The Surveillant Assemblage. *British Journal of Sociology* 51(4), 605–22.

Höller, H. P. and Wedde, P. (2018). Die Vermessung der Belegschaft. Mining the Enterprise Social Graph. *Mitbestimmungspraxis* 10. At www.boeckler.de/pdf/p_mbf_praxis_2018_010.pdf.

Holthaus, C., Park, Y. and Stock-Homburg, R. (2015). People Analytics und Datenschutz - Ein Widerspruch? *Datenschutz und Datensicherheit - DUD* 39, 676–81.

Huselid, M. (2018). The Science and Practice of Workforce Analytics: Introduction to the HRM Special Issue. *Human Resource Management* 57: 679–84.

Jain, N. and Maitri (2018). Big Data and Predictive Analytics: A Facilitator for Talent Management. In U. M. Munshi and N. Verma, eds. *Data Science Landscape*. Studies in Big Data 38. Singapore: Springer Nature, 199–204.

Khan, S. A. and Tang, J. (2017). The Paradox of Human Resource Analytics: Being Mindful of Employees. *Journal of General Management* 42(2), 57–66.

Lodge, D. and Mennicken, A. (2017). The Importance of Regulation of and by Algorithm. In L. Andrews et al., eds. *Algorithmic Regulation*, Centre for Analysis of Risk and Regulation at the London School of Economics and Political Science, pp. 2–6.

McDonald, P., Thompson, P. and O'Connor, P. (2016). Profiling Employees Online: Shifting Public-Private Boundaries in Organisational Life. *Human Resource Management* 26(4), 541–56.

MacKenzie, D. and Millo, Y. (2003). Constructing a Market, Performing Theory: The Historical Sociology of a Financial Derivatives Exchange. *American Journal of Sociology*, 109, 107–45.

Madsen, D. Ø. and Slåtten, K. (2017). The Rise of HR Analytics: A Preliminary Exploration. *Global Conference on Business and Finance Proceedings* 12(1), 148–59. At https://ssrn.com/abstract=2896602.

Manuti, A. and de Palma, P. D. (2018). *Digital HR: A Critical Management Approach to the Digitalization of Organizations*. Basingstoke: Palgrave Macmillan.

Marler, J. H. and Boudreau, J. W. (2017). An Evidence-Based Review of HR Analytics. *International Journal of Human Resource Management* 28(1), 3–26.

Minbaeva, D. B. (2018). Building Credible Human Capital Analytics for Organizational Competitive Advantage. *Human Resource Management* 57(3), 701–13.

Mishra, S., Raghvendra Lama, D. and Pal, Y. (2016). Human Resource Predictive Analytics (HRPA) for HR Management in Organizations. *International Journal of Scientific and Technology Research* 5(5), 33–5.

Moore, P. and Robinson, A. (2016). The Quantified Self: What Counts in the Neoliberal Workplace. *New Media & Society* 18(11), 2774–92.

Reindl, C. (2016). People Analytics: Datengestützte Mitarbeiterführung als Chance für die Organisationspsychologie. *Gruppe-Interaktion-Organisation* 47, 193–7.

Sousa, M. J. et al. (2019). Decision-Making Based on Big Data Analytics for People Management in Healthcare Organizations. *Journal of Medical Systems* 43(9):290.

Strohmeier, S. (2017). Big HR Data – Konzept zwischen Akzeptanz und Ablehnung. In W. Jochmann et al., eds. *HR-Exzellenz*. Wiesbaden: Springer, 339–55.

Sullivan, J. (2013). How Google Is Using People Analytics to Completely Reinvent HR. At www.tlnt.com/how-google-is-using-people-analytics-to-completely-reinvent-hr.

Swearingen, M. (2015). Share and Collaborate in the Enterprise with Office 365 Delve. At https://redmondmag.com/articles/2015/01/01/delve-into-enterprise-content.aspx.

Vormbusch, U. (2007). Eine Soziologie der Kalkulation. Werner Sombart und die Kulturbedeutung des Kalkulativen. In Hanno Pahl und Lars Meyer, eds. *Kognitiver Kapitalismus. Soziologische Beiträge zur Theorie der Wissensökonomie*. Marburg: Metropolis-Verlag, 75–96.

Vormbusch, U. (2009). Controlling the Future – Investing in People. Discussion Paper, presented at the London School of Economics and Political Science, Department of Accounting, 4 February 2009. At www.academia.edu/19467046/Talking_Numbers_-_Governing_Immaterial_Labour.

Vormbusch, U. (2020). Accounting For Who We Are and Could Be: Inventing Taxonomies of the Self in an Age of Uncertainty. In Andrea Mennicken and Robert Salais, eds. *The New Politics of Numbers*. Basingstoke: Palgrave Macmillan.

PART II

Faking It

6
Manufacturing Consent in the Gig Economy

Luca Perrig

Why do workers work as hard as they do? Following the work of Burawoy (1979), labour sociologists have extensively studied this question with regard to employment relationships. It is now widely acknowledged that a labour contract does not in itself suffice to enrol workers into an enterprise. Sophisticated management schemes have to be implemented in order to secure the workers' consent, most often by creating what Burawoy called an 'illusion of choice'. It is thus with great effort that managers channel the workers' force into value creation. The recent digitisation of work allows businesses to flourish by securing the consent of more workers. Most notably, gig-economy platforms have undertaken to automate management to justify their reliance on self-employed workers. The main challenge of this new form of management is twofold. First, the workforce is self-employed, which implies in particular that they should be legally allowed to set their own schedules and decline any job they are offered. The workers' enrolment is thus much more fragile since no employment contract can enforce even minimum consent. Second, the work is performed remotely, which implies that management must rely on smartphone apps to communicate. In this context, how do platforms manage to automate the manufacturing of gig workers' consent?

The control exerted by platforms in the gig economy is a topic that has already received considerable attention. It is common to every sector of the gig economy. Rosenblat (2018) has provided the first detailed account of algorithmic management with regard to the ride-hailing platforms. Wood et al. (2018) have recounted in detail the surveillance devices that micro-tasking platforms use. Ticona and Mateescu (2018) have shown that carework platforms create a form of visibility over which workers have no control, and thus contribute to enshrining existing inequalities. Cant (2020) has identified algorithmic management among the multiple 'systems of control' that Deliveroo uses on its workforce. What these insights have in common is that they are reported from below. They draw from interviews with workers and recount their experience of automated management. This chapter will provide a complementary insight by combining gig workers' experiences with accounts from the managers of food-delivery platforms. This perspective will allow us to sense the challenges that managers face by relying on a self-employed workforce. Gig work is a constant negotiation between workers and managers, who must convince workers not to reject the jobs they send (Shapiro 2018). We will see that data-driven management has its limits, and that platforms are often obliged to depart from their ideal role of mere intermediaries in order to facilitate transactions.

The remainder of the chapter is structured as follows. The next section will detail the data and methods used to conduct the study. Then, the main section of the chapter will discuss, in turn, three management devices that prove crucial in platform management: delivery fees, gamification and information. This will lead to a concluding discussion in the final section.

METHODOLOGY

This research draws from an ethnography of the online food-delivery market in Western-Switzerland that was conducted between August 2017 and December 2018. The fieldwork consisted in an engagement as a bike courier for five of the major platforms in the region for a period of six months. This participation provided opportunities for contact with numerous couriers, to study the app interface, and to observe workers in action as well as the interactions between managers and workers. This direct contact with couriers and managers also provided access to three instant messaging groups, which compiled a total of more than 10,000 messages. The next six months were devoted to the conduct of interviews with couriers (n=24) and managers (n=11) from four different platforms. Finally, I spent a month undertaking observations among managers inside the offices of a platform.

At the time of this study, food-delivery platforms in Switzerland were local and small-scale, operating with at most ten couriers working simultaneously. One multinational platform, Uber Eats, started its operations later during the timeframe of the study. This situation allowed an easier access to the inside of platform management since most headquarters were based in the region. It should be noted that these local platforms differ from multinational platforms most notably in their use of automation. While Uber Eats makes great use of sophisticated machine learning algorithms for its matching and pricing mechanisms, the other platforms studied here use at most simple algorithms that are configured 'by hand', which removes one layer of opacity and allows for a fruitful study (Burrell 2016). For the sake of anonymity, the platforms will be distinguished only when necessary in the remainder of this chapter.

THE TOOLS OF ACCEPTANCE

Delivering meals for an online platform involves long periods of waiting between orders. While waiting for work, couriers are typically outside, maybe close to a restaurant depending on their understanding of the matching algorithm. It is in these moments that the platform sends them what is legally equivalent to a job offer. The platform has to make these offers from afar, using the app to communicate. The tools at its disposal to frame this offer are limited and the decision must be quick. The offer thus typically consists of a screen displaying selected information about the task and a button on which the couriers can 'tap to accept'. We can identify three devices that platforms use to incentivise the couriers to accept the task: the delivery fees, gamification and information retention. Each will be addressed in turn.

Delivery fees

The delivery fees are the money that couriers get by accomplishing a delivery. They are set by the platform. There are numerous ways to set this payment: hourly pay, fixed piece rate, variable piece rate based on distance or any other criteria. However, platforms systematically choose a pricing scheme that supposedly provides the most incentives to workers. This reasoning is best displayed by one platform that tried to implement different pricing schemes before setting the usual distance-based delivery fee. The managers started by providing an hourly pay, but quickly reversed their decision, invoking biased incentives:

> 'It wasn't viable because some [couriers] slacked.'[1] (M1)

They then tried offering a fixed piece rate for each delivery, but this time acceptance was low and couriers started refusing tasks that were considered less valuable.

> 'They realised that it wasn't very fair because a courier that went far was paid the same rate as a courier with a shorter destination.' (M1)

By trial and error, these platform managers thus ended up implementing a payment scheme that would set different prices for each delivery according to the criteria that would most closely fit the couriers' preferences. However, they quickly realised how difficult this would be, since it required first having a good knowledge of the couriers' preferences and then being able to gather the data and put it into numbers. This leads most platforms to fix the delivery fee as a function of two factors: the distance and the moment of the delivery.

First, they take distance into account, often using the Google Maps API, which they realise is probably the most salient criterion. To implement this distance-dependent pricing, they set a base price, which is then incremented per radius of 2km around the restaurant. We should observe for now that this is a close approximation of the couriers' ideal, but the increment is made discrete and – most importantly – the distance between the couriers' current location and the restaurant is not taken into account. It is a complaint that managers hear about on a regular basis, but even though it would be technically possible for them to include it in the delivery fee, it would make previsions highly uncertain since the delivery fee would not be compensated by the price paid by the customers.

Second, the delivery fee is set to be a function of the moment at which the offer is made. Orders delivered on a Saturday or Sunday night will typically have higher delivery fees, up to twice as high as the delivery fee on a Monday afternoon. This partly responds to the couriers' reluctance to work late at night, but the price scheme is very grossly configured and while it provides incentives for couriers to log in at 7pm on a Saturday, many are still reluctant to accept a similar offer at 11pm.

1. Author's translations (from French).

Other more sophisticated platforms are able to include the weather into the frame and provide a fixed compensation per delivery in the case of heavy rain. Overall, at most three criteria are taken into account. In order to minimise the delivery fee while maximising the acceptance rate, platforms try to set a price that will reflect the couriers' preferences. But how exactly do couriers evaluate deliveries?

Couriers have a very clear view of what their ideal delivery would look like. Among the criteria that make for a good delivery, they mostly mention the following: the distance should not be too long, the itinerary should be flat, the weather nice, the meals should not be too heavy, no traffic jams, not too late at night, and the destination should be central. This implies that starting from a base delivery fee for this ideal delivery, every criterion that is not satisfied should be compensated by an increase in the delivery fee.

The pricing scheme thus falls short of the subtle appreciation couriers have of a given task. This unilateral and ill-defined pricing mechanism is part of the reason couriers are sometimes reluctant to accept a delivery. When couriers receive an offer whose itinerary goes up a hill, or meals that include heavy beverages, they are sometimes inclined to refuse it. Here is an excerpt from an interview that clearly shows the calculation couriers make:

> Author: 'Don't you get paid more if it's farther?'
> C1: 'That's bullshit! One franc, after one km! ... And the other thing is I [always check] the amount of the order. ... Once ... I had ten litres in my backpack!'

We can sense here the gap between the pricing that a platform sets and the courier's preferences. While platforms want to act as mere vehicles of preferences between buyers and sellers, they actually fall short of the market-clearing prices. Here lies a fundamental flaw that reveals the inability of platforms to perform as mere passive intermediaries. Much of the effort of platform management is thus devoted to making up for this imperfect pricing mechanism. Two devices will be leveraged in this regard: the implementation of gaming schemes and the retention of information about the deliveries.

Gamification

We saw that couriers will be more eager to accept jobs if the pay somewhat reflects the effort they estimate it will require. However, the limited data available to set these prices still leaves margin for improvement. One more device upon which platforms rely to gain the consent of couriers is to introduce gamification in the working process. Gamification in this context is a management practice that has little to do with playing, having more to do with incentivising by using soft nudges based on the collection of ranking points that resemble the design of traditional games. Following Woodcock and Johnson (2018), we thus use the term 'gamification' to refer to *gamification-from-above*. In our case, this will take the form of two devices: rankings and rewards.

The first, classical, way to incentivise workers is to rank them, display their performance publicly, and expect them to compete against each other for a small reward or just for the sake of competition. This device is widely used among food-delivery platforms. Performance ranking can come in many different forms. Couriers can be ranked according to their average speed, number of kilometres travelled, or number of stops. Figure 6.1 shows one such typical example. These rankings imply that work should be measured in some way, and this regularly comes with tensions as to the precise setting of the measurement devices. Couriers regularly seek to understand how the ranking is computed in order to behave accordingly. In one notable example, a platform sought to improve the transparency of its performance measures and sent a series of emails to its couriers giving details about the exact setting of the computation behind the measurement of the average speed. The message read as follows:

> Here is an explanation of how the [ranking] works:
> - we measure your location every 30 sec.
> - we measure the points between your stops only (so riding just for fun won't influence the results)
> - we measure the speed only when it is higher than 5 km/h and lower than 50 km/h. (M2)

These messages ultimately resulted in more confusion. Questions were raised about the measurement, most notably how short stops could be identified given that the app was measuring the average speed from recording the location only every 30 seconds. The managers wanted the couriers to be knowledgeable enough to participate in the game, but not so much that they would be able to 'game the system'.

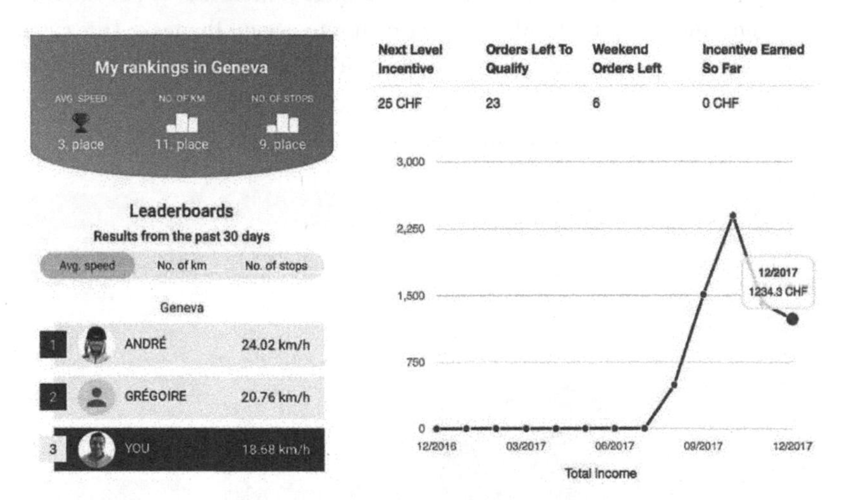

Figure 6.1 Gamification Devices: Rankings (left) And Bonuses (right)

Then, platforms also use bonuses as a form of gamification. Bonuses are typically given as a reward for attaining a given number of deliveries per week or month. Bonuses do not imply gamification per se, but platforms make a great amount of effort to display the bonuses as rewards for playing well. One notable feature of every food-delivery app is its dashboard. The dashboard is a screen where couriers can have access to their performance measures at one glance. The attainment of goals to earn bonuses is displayed here in order to convey a sense of urgency and prompt couriers to increase their acceptance rate. The screen on the right of Figure 6.1 shows one such dashboard, with a graph indicating the amount of deliveries per month and the 'orders left to qualify' for the next financial incentive.

Information

Communication about the job is the ultimate device platforms have at hand to obtain workers' consent. In order to evaluate an offer, couriers must be provided with information about the delivery. Only this will allow them to assess whether the price is worth the effort. The information provided by the platform is often very limited and can be presented on a single screen. Figure 6.2 shows screenshots of four apps at the moment the offer is made. When couriers receive an offer, this is the information that is provided to them and they have to decide whether or not to accept the task. This stage is the most important for platforms since it is by 'tapping to accept' that couriers become legally obliged to deliver the meal. What then is the information that couriers are provided with?

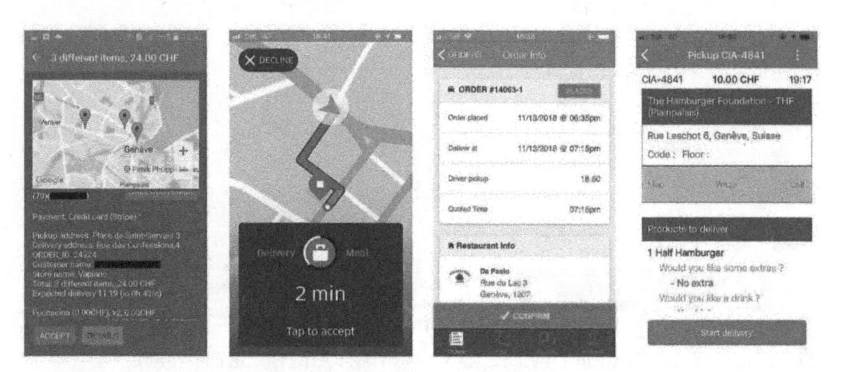

Figure 6.2 Information Available Before Accepting a Job Offer

First, let us consider the criterion that is most important according to couriers, which is the delivery fee. Most platforms do not provide any information about what couriers will earn once the order is completed. Only one platform displays a delivery fee (10CHF, on the rightmost screen in Figure 6.2). The others do not mention the delivery fees. One app provides the detailed route, from which a fee could be vaguely estimated, but most often couriers will have to assess the worth of a task without even knowing what they will earn. This prevents them from refusing deliveries that they may find worthless. For example, this is a manager reacting to a courier picking which deliveries to accept based on his past experience of delivery fees:

> 'The problem with him is that he calculates. He didn't know how delivery fees were set. But now he sees [Sushi Shop] and realises he can make money.' (M3)

This example shows how delivery fees are not aligned with couriers' preferences, which implies that transparent delivery fees could potentially give rise to couriers discriminating against certain deliveries.

The second most important criterion is information about the route. Couriers want to know the distance and location of both the restaurant and the customer in order to evaluate the task. The distance will be decisive since most bike couriers find long rides burdensome. The location of the restaurant is also a matter of concern since the ride between the courier's current location and the restaurant is not paid for by any platform. Couriers will thus resent accepting an order that asks them to ride a long distance to the restaurant. The customer's location will allow the couriers to have an idea of the quality of the route, if it is up a hill, if it goes through a busy neighbourhood, or if it is isolated so there will be few opportunities for receiving the next order in the vicinity. Information about the route varies greatly between platforms and is a good example of the power platforms have in deciding what information to provide. From our sample in Figure 6.2, we can observe that only the first app provides couriers with detailed information about the route. It has a map which displays current location, the restaurant and the final destination. The other three only provide information about the restaurant, so couriers know where to pick up the meal, but they have no clue about where they will be heading next.

Third, the weight and volume of the meal to be delivered can be critical for couriers in evaluating the drudgery of a delivery. Some managers thought about making this information available, but the task was considered technically too cumbersome for the little benefit it would provide.

> 'We thought about measuring the volume of every article, but it would be too complicated.' (M4)

Couriers will nonetheless try to estimate the weight from the menu details when available. From the number of items or the price of the meal to be delivered, it is possible to deduce the weight of a delivery. This will allow couriers to possibly decline an order that would require carrying a heavy meal, or drinks that could potentially be spilled in their bag. However, the information was here only inferred from a design feature that was not primarily intended for such use.

From these examples, we can see that platforms profit from their position as intermediaries by being able to thoroughly select the information that couriers will have available in their assessment of each job. This is a precious leverage for platforms that would like to make up for a price scheme that does not always provide adequate incentives. A typical example is the case of an order that is to be delivered quite far away. Such an order would probably come with a generous delivery fee because of the distance, but the price will not take into account whether the destination is in an isolated location or not. Couriers would discriminate against certain orders if they were provided with all the relevant information. Platforms thus withhold information in order to reduce the chances of this.

DISCUSSION

In this chapter, we have studied how platforms automate management by leveraging delivery fees, gamification, and the provision of information to enrol workers into as many transactions as possible. Two questions remain open for discussion. What are the effects of this automation on the work that couriers provide? What does it imply for the study of the gig economy?

The efficacy of platform management is difficult to assess. During interviews, couriers regularly denied that the incentives had any effect on their acceptance rate. Most mentioned financial imperatives as the main factor driving their decisions, implying that they would accept any order they were offered regardless of the delivery fee, distance, bonus or any other criterion. They just needed the money and being picky would have been a luxury. However, later in the interviews, couriers would often mention 'this one time' it snowed / they were eating / it was late / they bumped into a friend, and the order they received suddenly seemed worthless. Consider the following remark addressing the influence of bonuses:

> 'If your shift ends at 6pm and you receive an order at 5:55pm, would you take it? Well if it's the 15th, you take it [and get a bonus]. If it's the 8th, you might think "I have other plans", and refuse it.' (C2)

Even though, overall, couriers are mainly driven by financial necessity, platforms rely on these incentives to increase the acceptance rate at the margins. This hold on the deliveries that are most delicate to secure will prove essential in the competition among platforms. As such, it becomes crucial to include the tools of platform management in the framework of analysis to understand the labour market that platforms organise. The data that is gathered as well as the algorithms that process it allow platforms to exert considerable control (Lee et al. 2015). From our observations, we can distinguish two ways in which markets are affected by platform management.

First, the quantity of labour provided by couriers is best understood as arising from their enrolment by the platform. Far from merely providing an intermediation device between supply and demand, platforms act upon the quantity of labour on many levels. Be it through the pricing scheme, information retention, or gamification, the platform enrols its workforce in a way that is reminiscent of the marketing techniques that are used to seduce its customers. The ultimate quantity of labour that is provided in this market is thus less the result of an equilibrium than of asymmetries embedded in the working tools (Rosenblat and Stark 2016).

Second, the prices in this labour market are dependent on the measurement tools accessible to the platform. Far from representing the ideal equilibrium price that algorithms are supposedly able to compute, the delivery fee that couriers are granted is based on the data that platforms are able to gather. The price of a delivery is thus set according to a limited range of criteria such as distance, time and weather, each of which is approximated using the available computational tools. The estimation of the couriers' propensity to work gives rise to a complex game of evaluation between platforms and couriers in assessing the worth of a delivery. By studying this game our analysis has led to a thorough understanding of price setting in the food-delivery market. On the one hand, managers try to anticipate the workers' preferences, on the other hand couriers behave according to the information the app affords.

What this detailed inquiry has revealed is that market intermediaries play a crucial role in the shaping of markets, and that studying them is best achieved by looking at the tools they provide to the actors involved. The gig economy is an ideal case study for such an endeavour, since it undertakes to build labour markets from top to bottom.

REFERENCES

Burawoy, M. (1979). *Manufacturing Consent*. Chicago: University of Chicago Press.

Burrell, J. (2016). How the Machine 'Thinks': Understanding Opacity in Machine Learning Algorithms. *Big Data & Society* 3(1), 1–12.

Cant, C. (2020). *Riding for Deliveroo: Resistance in the New Economy.* Cambridge: Polity.

Lee, M. K., Kusbit, D., Metsky, E. and Dabbish, L. (2015). Working with Machines: The Impact of Algorithmic and Data-Driven Management on Human Workers. *Proceedings of the 33rd Annual ACM Conference on Human Factors in Computing Systems*, 1603–12.

Rosenblat, A. (2018). *Uberland: How Algorithms are Rewriting the Rules of Work.* Berkeley: University of California Press.

Rosenblat, A. and Stark, L. (2016). Algorithmic Labor and Information Asymmetries: A Case Study of Uber's Drivers. *International Journal of Communication* 10, 3758–84.

Shapiro, A. (2018). Between Autonomy and Control: Strategies of Arbitrage in the 'on-Demand' Economy. *New Media & Society* 20(8), 2954–71.

Ticona, J. and Mateescu, A. (2018). Trusted Strangers: Carework Platforms' Cultural Entrepreneurship in the On-Demand Economy. *New Media & Society* 20(11), 4384–404.

Wood, A. J., Graham, M., Lehdonvirta, V. and Hjorth, I. (2018). Good Gig, Bad Gig: Autonomy and Algorithmic Control in the Global Gig Economy. *Work, Employment and Society* 33(1), 56–75.

Woodcock, J. and Johnson, M. R. (2018). Gamification: What It Is, and How to Fight It. *The Sociological Review* 66(3), 542–58.

7

Automated and Autonomous? Technologies Mediating the Exertion and Perception of Labour Control

Beatriz Casas González

The question about the relationship between technological change and labour autonomy is a constant in the sociology of work and the object of a large number of empirical studies. The answers to that question vary to a great extent, from authors emphasising the technological potential for labour's empowerment, work relief, up- and multi-skilling, to others concerned about increased labour control, deskilling and job destruction. The ongoing digitalisation of work has recently revived this debate, with a current tendency to assess the impact of digitalisation on labour autonomy in terms of its consequences for workers' scope of action.

The empirical insights our research team gathered between 2017 and 2019 – through 47 qualitative interviews with production workers, technologists, management and employees' representatives from two manufacturing companies in the electronic and communication technologies industry in Germany – offer a new perspective on this question.[1] They point towards a widespread sense of autonomy among workers whose labour activity is prescribed and monitored through different technologies, mainly assistance systems, Enterprise Resource Planning (ERP) and real-time tracking technologies.

In our research we found that these technologies, in interaction with the mode(s) of labour control operating in the workplace, can influence workers' agency in a twofold way: in some cases, the use of technologies is inscribed into a strategy of direct labour control, thus limiting workers'

1. The research was conducted within the framework of the SOdA-Project, led by the ISF Munich and funded by the German Ministry of Education and Research.

scope of action and decision. In other cases, technologies are used as part of a strategy of control relying upon the demand for and expansion of workers' agency – obviously only to the extent and under the conditions that make the functioning of this control strategy possible. Both modes of labour control tend to coexist in the same workplace. This might lead to contradictions and strains, which workers often have to solve on their own.

Interestingly, according to our empirical insights, workers do not seem to associate either the techno-organisational restriction of their scope of action nor the technologically supported instrumentalisation of their agency with greater labour control. This finding motivated me to explore circumstances under which workers' perceptions of control are formed. Moreover, it suggested the need to draw attention towards the subjective influence of technologies as a potential key factor in the formation of workers' perception of labour control.

In this chapter I present some aspects of my ongoing PhD research on technologically mediated influence over workers' perceptions of control. After sketching the context of this empirical problem, I shall discuss the following questions: (How) does the use of technologies affect the way labour control is exerted over and perceived by workers? And how do these perceptions relate to the reproduction of capital's domination in the workplace?

LABOUR ORGANISATION IN THE PLANTS INVESTIGATED

Company A[2]

Company A is a manufacturing plant of a larger, non-listed family business headquartered in Germany. The company's business segment comprises the area of radio and measurement technology, and it addresses primarily major customers from the trade and public sectors. In addition to the actual production, the product and service portfolio also includes services such as system design and on-site customer briefing.

The plant under review is one of three manufacturing plants of the company and a member of the limited liability structure. It operates as an 'in-house service provider', primarily in the field of secure communication systems.

2. Both companies have been anonymised for data privacy reasons.

Compared to other companies in the industry, Company A faces a low market pressure and its scope of operations is relatively large. However, the tendency marked by the new area management points towards more budget controlling. This limits the scope of action of both the plant and its departments, and places a greater emphasis on cost efficiency and entrepreneurship throughout all plant levels.

Company A employs approximately 1,700 persons in total, 4 per cent of which occupy managerial positions. Among production workers, 40 per cent are considered skilled and 15 per cent semi-skilled workers. The rest are engineers and technicians. Regarding the gender composition, women make up 25 per cent of the employees, and 3 per cent of the managers. Two thirds of the total labour force is employed in production, and one third in administration. Between 30 and 40 per cent of the production workers have temporary contracts, with a recently concluded company agreement envisaging 250 successive temporary contracts.

The factory's hierarchy has three levels: plant manager, department manager and group leader. The density of the union, IG Metall, is around 20 per cent in production. Salaries are based on working time plus a performance bonus. A company agreement for flexible salary adjustment to the plant's target achievement is currently in force. As a result, approximately two thirds of the compulsory overtime is paid to the workers, and the other third remains unpaid. Depending on the order situation, overtime and Saturday work can be widespread, but, as all participants stress, on a 'strictly voluntary' basis. As this applies not least to temporary workers, voluntariness always remains two-edged. The flextime account is formally limited to 250 hours. However, the existence of an additional long-term account means that virtually no limit is set to possible fluctuations in working hours. Production workers organise their working time in consultation with the group leader or even team spokespersons and colleagues, often largely self-responsible.

The company's organisational structure is divided into nine departments. Three departments are responsible for the prefabrication works (machining technology, housing production and printed circuit board production) and another three deal with the final production area (processing and assembly). There is a service department, another for human resources, and the 'lean department', which is directly subordinate to the plant management.

Company B

Company B manufactures complex printed circuit boards and components as well as switch cabinets for the branches of safety, medical and industrial control. The company is a so-called Electronic Manufacturing Service (EMS) provider, specialising in cost-intensive, custom-made products and in finding technical solutions, including in development and production. Company B has evolved from a classic manufacturing operation into a Joint Development Manufacturing (JDM) partner. This means that it supports customers not only in the production of electronic assemblies and customised systems, but also in product development.

Company B faces a fiercely contested market: According to the managing director, in Germany alone there are between 300 and 400 EMS service providers with which they compete. With its size (150 employees), the company is in the midfield of EMS companies. Moreover, they are in competition with EMS providers from Eastern Europe and Asia too.

Salaries are based on working time plus a personal performance bonus of 5 per cent, which is paid out depending on subjective performance evaluation. A profit share of 10 per cent for all employees exists formally, but has not been distributed in the last few years, as company B did not generate profits.

Employees are hired on the basis of a 35-hour, six-day week. Two Saturdays a month are compulsory. In overload situations, workers perform additional Saturday work. This is, according to the management, on a 'voluntary basis' and paid with an additional 25 per cent. From the employees' perspective, the degree of voluntariness is relative, in a context of omnipresent job insecurity.

Production is divided into four departments, each of them dealing with an area of production. Every department has between five and eight employees in administration and between eight and 20 in production, and is led by a production manager. Although each department is largely self-sufficient and has its own developers, technologists, etc., there is still a superordinate and not production-related technology department. This should rather be located on the entrepreneur side and fulfils a 'cross function'. Thus, for instance, the technology department is responsible for assessing the technical and organisational feasibility of customer requests, developing technical solutions, providing the management with the information necessary for the preparation of customer offers, etc. It is also the technology department that sets the time required for every step in the production process. The price of the customer offers include, alongside fixed costs for materials, the cost of production's labour time. Management's strategy consists in shortening the estimated labour time to reduce the offers' price and thus enhance the company's market competitiveness. For production workers this means often having to stick to unrealistic target times, and increasingly leads to conflicts between technology and production.

This brief glimpse into both companies shows how labour organisation, alongside other factors – such as workers' job insecurity resulting both from their employment status and the company's market position – restricts the autonomy of workers on fundamental questions such as working time. There are further ways in which workers' autonomy is constrained, for example through their interaction with technology, as we shall see below. But workers in these companies not only face restrictions on their scope of action. Managers rely for different reasons on workers' agency and self-responsibility too, and I will argue that technology can be key also in instrumentalising workers' autonomy.

THE INFLUENCE OF TECHNOLOGIES ON THE EXERTION AND PERCEPTION OF LABOUR CONTROL

Framing the theoretical debate

The relationship between technology, labour control and capital's domination in the workplace is a classical problem in the critical sociology of work. Today, the ubiquitous presence of 'digitalisation' in public and academic debates has given renewed momentum to this question, as evidenced by the recent discussion on 'digital Taylorism'. Nonetheless, as I will argue here, both current and classical accounts miss what I see as a key aspect of capital's domination in the workplace, namely, the link between technology and worker's subjective perceptions of control.

Since its origins in the late 1970s, the question of the implications of technology for workers' scope of action and, more generally, for labour control has marked the Labour Process (LP) debates. Back then, the critique of Braverman's thesis in *Labor and Monopoly Capital* (1974) – that technology's design and use in the labour process responded to a management strategy of labour intensification and degradation – led to the so-called second wave of Labour Process Theory (LPT).[3] Here the discussion revolved around the dialectics of 'deskilling versus responsible autonomy and coercion versus consent' (Vidal 2018). Against Braverman's thesis, authors like Friedman (1977) and Burawoy (1979, 1985) highlighted the relevance of workers' subjectivity for corporate goals. For Burawoy, what ensured a high level of productivity in his case studies was not direct and coercive control, but workers' active cooperation in the production process, achieved through shopfloor-induced 'games' of 'making-out'. Thus, he showed how generating workers' active consent via the expansion of their self-organisation can be crucial for capital's dominance. The issue of subjectivity continued to feed subsequent LP debates; Knights (1990) and Willmott (1990) saw Burawoy's work as a first yet insufficient step towards a theory of the subject. They criticised LP accounts as widely trapped in some variant of objectivism – thus overlooking subjectivation – or, at best, in a binary opposition between 'free' subjects and 'oppressive' structures. The reactions to those criticisms (cf. Thompson and O'Doherty 2009) resulted in the third LP wave, and the controversy is still unresolved.

A somewhat similar thesis to Braverman's can be found today in the discussion of 'digital Taylorism'. The term is used to refer to a mode of control characterised, like its classical counterpart, by coercion, the restriction of labour's scope of action and subjectivity, and the division between conception and execution. Technical applications – such as real-time tracking and tracing, digitally supported assistance systems and automation – enable this great control scenario by offering new possibilities for labour deskilling, fragmentation and the standardisation of labour processes, etc. (cf. Brown, Lauder and Ashton 2011; Nachtwey and Staab 2015; Altenried 2017; Butollo et al. 2018). Against the digital Taylorist approach some authors have pointed to its several limitations: First, its almost exclusive focus on specific sectors of contemporary capitalist economies – mostly logistics and crowdwork – gives rise to questions about whether its empirical results may be extrapolated to the sphere of production or other sectors of the economy. Second, it assumes restrictive labour control as the sole or main interest of management, thus overlooking activating forms of labour control and other interests behind digitalisation strategies (cf. Menz and Nies 2019). Therefore, digital

3. For a detailed categorisation of the different Labour Process Theory waves see Thompson and O'Doherty 2009.

Taylorism's view of subjectivity as disruptive for labour control prevents it from taking into account the role of workers' subjectivities for the exercise of capital's domination in the workplace. Moreover, its approach to technology's subjective effects only in terms of restriction hinders its capacity to consider other forms of technological influence, such as technology's impact on workers' subjective perceptions of control.

By asking how these perceptions are formed in interaction with technology in the labour process, and how they relate to the reproduction of capital's domination in the workplace, I aim to contribute to what is, following Thompson and O'Doherty (2009), still LPT's pending task: bringing the subject into a materialist analysis of the changing political economy of capitalism.

Framing the empirical problem

In the case studies considered here, we find examples of digital technologies used both as part of coercive control strategies and in the production of workers' consent. Interestingly, despite the technologically mediated constriction and/or instrumentalisation of their agency, workers in these companies to a large extent share a strong sense of autonomy. In the remainder of this chapter I shall address this apparent contradiction, starting by introducing some extracts from our interviews with production workers in both companies. These aim to illustrate how labour control is currently exerted and perceived by workers in these workplaces, and the role played by different technologies, like Enterprise Resource Planning (ERP), real-time tracking and assistance systems.

The following case of a circuit board assembler from the EMS company offers a good example of how the use of technology in the labour process can place significant restrictions on workers' scope of action, which, however, are not felt as such. This worker told us that she now has a greater sense of freedom than in her former job as a saleswoman in a bakery, since she no longer has to deal with customers' complaints about things she can't do anything about:

> 'In my previous job as a bakery saleswoman I just had to deal with customers all day … I mean, there were a lot of nice customers, but also customers who you had to justify yourself to for things you could not do

> anything about. Yes, it just was not fun anymore … You don't have that here. I definitely feel freer here.'

Interestingly, when she explained to us her interaction with the so-called 'royonic table' – an assistance system with which she carries out the circuit board assembly – it became clear that it is a very technically determined activity, allowing for no variations or improvisation in the assembly process:

> 'Yeah, so I put my circuit board here like that. Then I have a screen, a beam of light at the top, and here I have my components in the table. There are five different boxes in a row, and then I have a foot pedal here, or with my hand I can push further. On the screen I get to see with a beam of light where the component is going: top left, and this reference point shows me: right there. The beam of light then shines onto the circuit board. The box with the component opens, and then here the beam of light lights up on the corner where you have to place it. It also shows me the pole. If the component has polarity, then it flashes exactly where the polarity is, and if the component has no polarity, then it does not blink.'

In my view, this case is a paradigmatic example of *technologically mediated direct control*. Here, labour control is allocated to technology itself, by constraining workers' agency through their interaction with the assistance system. Yet this worker feels 'definitely freer now'. How is this possible?

The reason, I argue, is that the rational and objective character ascribed to technology can make technologically mediated control seem fairer and more accurate to the workers than arbitrary and fallible personal rule – be it from customers or supervisors.

We found a similar phenomenon when asking workers from the same company for their opinion on the introduction of new terminals that would help managers trace in real-time their individual location and performance. The workers we interviewed welcomed this initiative on the grounds of 'accuracy'. This suggests that such a view of technology can provide technological mediated control with a source of legitimacy, and render its effects unproblematic in the eyes of the workers. This can be seen in the following interview extract with another circuit board assembler:

> Interviewer (IV): And with the new terminals is it now possible to retrace in more detail what you individually have been doing throughout the day?
> Worker (W): Yes, for the area manager in any case.
> IV: Is that problematic or does it not matter?
> W: No, not at all ... No, I just think it's fair, because that's accurate.

However, the use of this form of real-time tracing can also offer a tool for workers to defend their performance against managers. This is especially true in the case of the EMS company, whose situation of fierce market competition is passed on to production workers in the form of high productivity pressure, as we saw in the previous section. In this context, workers perceive these new terminals as a chance to prove their actual work to managers, as a milling worker from the company explained to us:

> 'I do not think it [the introduction of the new terminals] is wrong, let's say so ... At least it shows that I did not sit around twiddling my thumbs in that time, instead he sees: aha, she did something for SMD or for the test field.'

There are also scenarios where technology is not inscribed within a mode of direct control, thus limiting workers' agency. It can also serve a strategy of indirect control, which relies on technology for capital's instrumentalisation of workers' subjectivity.[4]

This is indeed the case at the TV and broadcast manufacturing company, where workers are self-responsible for introducing different data related to their own performance and the status of the labour process in the ERP system. For instance, they record information on their attendance hours, what orders they've processed and how long it took them to do so, what orders are still pending, etc. Through the ERP, workers' performance is digitally monitored and translated into digital indicators, like the so-called 'intensity level'. This represents the ratio between attendance and productive hours in a day, measured on the basis of the estimated processing time for each order. Since workers record this information under their username, their individual performance could be re-traced by a person with access to

4. The distinction between direct and indirect control is however not always clearly defined in the praxis, and we often find a combination of both in one and the same workplace.

this data, as a system assembly worker explained to us. Whether and how the data about her performance is used is outside her knowledge, but this does not seem to worry her:

> IV: Does anyone do that [re-trace your performance data]?
> W: No Idea. [laughs]
> IV: So, you don't fear anything?
> W: No. Actually, not.

This was not just a single case. Most workers in the company assumed and expected that their performance could be technologically monitored, but whether and how exactly this happened was unknown to them. As a logistics worker put it:

> 'I assume our team spokesman controls whether I've done my job or not. I don't know, though.'

ERP systems, therefore, give both managers and workers information about the status of the production process and workers' individual performance. In that sense, ERP technologies are key mediators between management and production. But these technologies do more than just provide information. In the specific mode of control where the interaction between workers and ERP systems takes place, these technologies have the capacity to influence workers' actions and agency. The form of this influence is twofold: On the one hand, it restricts workers' scope for action and decision-making with regards to their work activity. Workers are prescribed through the ERP system what job they have to do, when, for how long, etc. On the other hand, the use of this technology demands workers' agency to access the information, enter the personal data and evaluate digitally generated data. Thus, I argue that the use of ERP systems is inscribed within a rationalisation strategy, directed both towards the labour process and the labour force, where activation and restriction of workers' agency coexist. In other words, ERP supports both the regulation of the labour process and workers' self-regulation, allowing – at least partially – for a technological reallocation of managerial functions from managers to workers themselves.

As a result of technological mediation, personal supervision becomes increasingly redundant. This can create the impression among workers that no control is being exerted on them, or at least make it hardly identifiable, as this extract from our interview with an electroplating worker shows:

> IV: How is it controlled at all? How does your supervisor know that you are doing what you should do?
> W: To be honest, I do not see my supervisor all week. [laughs]
> IV: Exactly, but how does he know you're working?
> W: I do not know ...

Moreover, the fact that performance requirements are transmitted to workers through technology – in this case, via the ERP – can lead to the impression that these demands come from the ERP system itself. In this way, the market relations, and the relations between workers and management that lie behind these performance requirements, are rendered invisible through the mediation of technology. The following extract from an interview with a logistics worker illustrates this idea:

> IV: Where does the workload come from?
> W: We're in the shipping, that means, we get ... three times a day the commission lists are printed and that's the stuff that should go out.
> IV: Who enters this?
> W: That comes from the system.

All these examples point towards a highly interesting effect of technologically mediated labour control, namely, a fetishisation of technology. By this I mean a subjective perception that consists of the mystification and disguise of the unequal social relations underlying technology's design and use, and its implications for labour control. Technology's fetishisation can lead, as we have seen, to legitimising labour control and rendering it unproblematic, or making it and the broader social relations around it hardly identifiable.

CONCLUSIONS

As I have argued in this chapter, the use of technologies in the labour process is a key factor, but not the only one, that influences workers' agency. The sense of this influence is neither univocal nor linear. It depends to a great extent on what technology is being used, and as part of what mode of control: either direct and constraining or indirect and activating. In the first case, control is allocated to technology itself (e.g. the 'royonic table'), by restricting workers' scope of action. In the latter case, a (partial) reallocation of managerial functions from management to workers takes place. Here, the use of technology (e.g. ERP) demands workers' subjectivity and is meant to support its instrumentalisation by capital.

Despite these differences, the empirical examples I have presented point towards a common effect of the use of technologies in the labour process: At the organisational level, it affects, in one way or another, how labour control is exerted. At a subjective level, it has an influence on how control is perceived. As labour control becomes increasingly depersonalised and/or internalised through technological mediation, it can be legitimised or obscured based on a fetishised perception of technology; that is, on the illusion of a socially neutral, infallible and objective technology that disguises the unequal social relations and conflicting interests underlying its very design and use.

However, technological fetishisation is only one among other potential subjective effects of the interaction between workers and digital technologies in the labour process. There are other possible scenarios which, far from supporting relations of accumulation and power, might threaten them, for instance by revealing internal contradictions and breakpoints. Given the increasing relevance of digital technologies in production processes, the question of technology's effects on workers' perceptions of control is key for understanding how the reproduction of capital's domination works today, and how it can eventually be disrupted.

REFERENCES

Altenried, M. (2017). Die Plattform als Fabrik. Crowdwork, Digitaler Taylorismus und die Vervielfältigung der Arbeit. *PROKLA* 47(187), 175–91.

Braverman, H. (1974). *Labor and Monopoly Capital*. New York: Monthly Review Press.

Brown, P., Lauder, H. and Ashton, D. N. (2011). The Global Auction: The Broken Promises of Education, Jobs, and Incomes. *Perspectives* 16(3).

Burawoy, M. (1979). *Manufacturing Consent*. Chicago: University of Chicago Press.

Burawoy, M. (1985). *The Politics of Production*. London: Verso.

Butollo, F., Engel, T., Füchtenkötter, M., Koepp R. and Ottaiano, M. (2018). Wie stabil ist der digitale Taylorismus? Störungsbehebung, Prozessverbesserungen und Beschäftigungssystem bei einem Unternehmen des Online-Versandhandels. *AIS Studien* 11(2), 143–59.

Friedman, A. L. (1977). *Industry and Labour: Class Struggle at Work and Monopoly Capitalism*. London: Macmillan.
Knights, D. (1990). Subjectivity, Power and the Labour Process. In D. Knights and H. Willmott, eds. *Labour Process Theory*. London: Macmillan, 297–335.
Menz, W. and Nies, S. (2019). Autorität, Markt und Subjektivität: Ergebnisse einer sekundäranalytischen Längsschnittstudie vom Spät-Taylorismus bis zur Digitalisierung der Arbeit. In W. Dunkel, N. Mayer-Ahuja and H. Hanekop, eds. *Blick zurück nach vorn. Sekundäranalysen zum Wandel von Arbeit nach dem Fordismus*. Frankfurt am Main: Campus, 175–217.
Nachtwey, O. and Staab, P. (2015). Die Avantgarde des digitalen Kapitalismus. *Mittelweg* 36 24(6), 59–84.
Thompson, P. and O'Doherty, D. (2009). Perspectives on Labor Process Theory. In M. Alvesson, T. Bridgman and H. Willmott, eds. *The Oxford Handbook of Critical Management Studies*. Oxford: Oxford University Press, 99–121.
Vidal, M. (2018). Work and Exploitation in Capitalism: The Labor Process and the Valorization Process. In M. Vidal, P. Prew, T. Rotta and T. Smith, eds. *Oxford Handbook of Karl Marx*. New York: Oxford University Press, 241–60.
Willmott, H. C. (1990). Subjectivity and the Dialectics of Praxis: Opening up the Core of Labour Process Analysis. In D. Knights and H. Willmott, eds. *Labour Process Theory*. London: Macmillan, 336–78.

8

Can Robots Produce Customer Confidence? Contradictions Among Automation, New Mechanisms of Control and Resistances in the Banking Labour Process

Giorgio Boccardo

An extensive transformation of financial intermediation services has been seen in recent years. Concepts such as digital platforms, business intelligence, mobile apps, digital banking or virtual office have been increasingly implemented within the Chilean banking sector. For supporters of technological change, this is about a local adaptation to the global financial market, greater possibilities for innovation, and the creation of skilled jobs. On the other hand, opponents depict this scenario as creating a massive extinction of job positions, less social security and more labour uncertainty. Beyond these perspectives, however, it is an undeniable fact that the banking labour process is being transformed at a staggering speed.

Automation is not a new topic in relation to the changes the banking labour process is going through. In fact, it is a secular trend that has evidenced specific features over the last six decades. However, in the last decade, the sharp transformation of the global labour process has reopened a debate on key issues such as the end of work, which occupations will be automated, new mechanisms of control and forms of worker resistance, and what defines the current automation process (Brynjolfsson and McAfee 2014; Srnicek and Williams 2015; Briken, Chillas and Krzywdzinski 2017).

In the banking labour process, these changes have automated several jobs such as those of cashiers, client services and telephone executives. In other cases, routine tasks have been replaced; nevertheless, it has proven more difficult to substitute skills related to human relationships. In this sense, automation in the banking labour process (through robots and computerisation of procedures) depends on work skills but also on degrees of confidence between bank workers and customers. In any case, the introduction of new technologies is changing the mechanisms of control in banks. While in the workplace, new kinds of worker resistance arise.

This raises questions about whether automation is inevitable. Does it necessarily mean the end of banking occupations? Is this the beginning of a fully digital banking system? What are the consequences for workers and what can their trade unions do about it?

The aim of this chapter is to explain the contradictions among automation, new mechanisms of control and resistances, and the construction of customer confidence in the Chilean banking labour process. The introduction of new technologies within the banking labour process are explored; modern kinds of control, labour deskilling and upskilling, and resistance as a result of such new technologies are analysed; finally, there is a reflection on banking automation boundaries and possibilities in relation to the reproduction of confidence between banking institutions and their clients.

The study used exploratory mixed methods research design.[1] The results presented here are based on an analysis of labour market trends in banking intermediation services (2005–18) with data taken from the Superintendence of Banks and Financial Institutions (SBIF); 36 in-depth interviews conducted with workers, supervisors and trade union leaders – according to gender and experience – in a large Chilean bank; and an eight-year ethnographic work in a bank trade union. Specifically, the in-depth interviews and ethnography were completed in one large private bank controlled by Chilean capitals (1st in number of workers and 2nd in economic profit in 2018). The Chilean banking labour process case shows characteristics common to many other countries – in terms of higher organisational and salary flexibility, lower numerical flexibility, trade union tradition, and feminisation of the labour process.

CHILEAN BANKING: AN INDUSTRY IN CONSTANT AUTOMATION

Historically speaking, and in relation to other productive sectors, banking has pioneered the introduction of technology for the organisation of its

1. The research was funded by the National Grant for Doctorate (CONICYT) No. 21161233.

labour process (Sathye 1999; Sadovska and Kamola 2017). The first records of this in the Chilean case are found back in the 1960s with the arrival of computers to manage clients' bank accounts, debt collection, accounts systems and financial statistics on a centralised basis (Mella and Parra 1990). By the end of the 1970s, the foreign and domestic banking system was interconnected by the Society for Worldwide Interbank Financial Telecommunication (SWIFT), and automated reply devices plus call centres for client service were introduced. During the 1980s and early '90s, the computerisation of financial processes in offices via 24/7 transactions and online transfers between branches and banks started, and some occupations were automated by ATMs. In the 2000s, institutional webpages with a variety of online services were created, and the coverage and services given by telephone banking were expanded.

All these technological transformations suppressed both skilled and deskilled occupations and/or replaced routine specific tasks; in addition, control mechanisms as well as resistances within the banking labour process were transformed. However, the dramatic financialisation that Chilean society has experimented with in recent decades (Moulian 1997), with the growth of consumer loans and the commodification of basic goods such as education, health or retirement funds (Ruiz and Boccardo 2014), resulted in increasing demand for banking services, while the positions on which this relies were becoming obsolete (Mauro 2004).

After the severe economic crisis of 2008, the banking industry introduced new technologies for the rearrangement of the labour process, aiming to increase its strength. Massive data mining of clients, increased computerisation of administrative procedures and telephone banking, and the sale of products through multiple digital channels began to articulate an innovative banking scheme increasingly oriented towards the 'production' of customised financial services according to the clients' particular needs.

In this respect, the automation of occupations and tasks has been a constant in financial intermediation services (Frías 1990). What then is the original feature of the most recent automation wave? Who is being affected by these transformations, and how?

From 2015 onwards, a variety of indicators show an absolute reduction of the banking labour force; i.e. the extinction rate is bigger than the rate of new occupations created. Nevertheless, unlike the crises in 1997 or 2008, this change cannot be directly linked to the economic situation (Boccardo 2019).

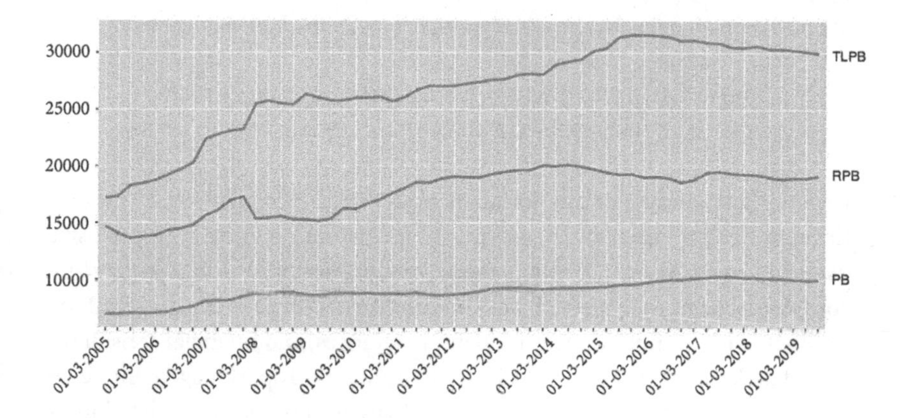

Figure 8.1 Banking Employees (2005–2018)
Source: Author's analysis based on SBIF data.

Figure 8.1 shows the decrease of the banking labour force[2] in absolute terms. In fact, in recent years, the number of employees has decreased strongly within the three largest private banks[3] (TLPD) and more slowly in the rest of the private banks (RPB). By contrast, in the public bank (PB) the rise of the banking labour force has stagnated. Private banks introduced new technologies on an intensive basis and began a dramatic automation of their offices, whereas the public bank remained more steady, although in 2018 it too began to join this tendency. In addition, in the last four years, 1,181 positions directly connected to financial institutions were removed, which is an indicator of a gradually intensified reduction trend.

Attributing these changes in the banking industry only to the automation of tasks and occupations does not give rise to an adequate understanding of such a complex issue. Firstly, because the main characteristics result from a combination of new technologies (Kalleberg 2001; Boccardo 2013), a growing feminisation of occupations (Crompton 1989; Riquelme 2013), and

2. Direct banking employees of Headquarters, Branches, Auxiliary Boxes and Support Offices are considered.
3. In September 2019, TLPB concentrated 54.1% of current accounts and 65.9% of amounts in national currency, and 49.9% of loans.

the actions of trade unions (Mauro 2004; Narbona 2012). Secondly, because the recent evidence shows that new technologies are eliminating a bounded proportion of occupations and/or tasks as well as increasing labour deskilling and control over the remaining employees in the banking industry.

THE BANKING LABOUR PROCESS: AUTOMATION, NEW MECHANISMS OF CONTROL AND RESISTANCES

Banking has always had as its main objective the acquisition of income through the provision of financial intermediation services. The intensive use of its main assets – namely, money and information – has triggered a complex labour process which aims to reconstruct those assets into banking products such as money custody, loans, insurances, and financial consultancies of all kinds (Frías 1990). In order to do so, the Top Management Team must articulate three different areas of 'banking production' – headquarter and administrative offices, physical branches or offices, and telephone banking. However, the three processes have a common denominator, which is the production and reproduction of confidence between clients and the banking institution.

Headquarter and administrative offices is the area where skilled and semi-skilled workers are located, such as division managers, internal process supervisors, programmers, data analysts, product designers and administrative staff. They work on the management and reproduction of the confidence of institutional clients and financial markets, clients' data mining, financial services and product design, plus the exercise of internal control. In the headquarters, skilled workers have meaningful levels of autonomy, while bureaucratic control predominates in administrative offices.

In recent years, the appearance of 'Business Intelligence' departments has been radically transforming the financial business. New banking makes use of diverse digital platforms for the collection of clients' data and its subsequent exploitation by machine learning for a deeper comprehension of their consumption needs. Consumer market hyper-segmentation strategies have also been created in order to provide financial consultancy to institutional clients and wealthy families. These recently introduced units gradually replace skilled occupations such as programmers and data analysts with others whose skills better fit the new productive process. However, commercial executives working in offices and telephone executives are also affected, since such units 'make the decision' on the products to be offered to each client. In the words of an experienced banking trade-union leader, 'The Business Intelligence unit provides the commercial executives a database of pre-approved loans which are otherwise offered directly on the website or mobile apps.'

Banking offices employ semi-skilled workers such as office agents, management chiefs, commercial executives, cashiers, public service staff and guards. The work here involves the sale of financial products, administration of clients' portfolios, sales and assistance for the general public, and financial consultancy for private clients and companies. The key to carrying out these activities is the mastering of emotional and aesthetic skills managed on an organisational basis (Thompson, Warhurst and Callaghan 2001) to produce and reproduce confidence in face-to-face relations between clients and the banking institutions. As one experienced commercial executive put it: the key is 'the sympathy you had with the client. While talking to them, you asked "why do you want it?" and they told you their stories. Then, you created the confidence bond with the client.' In fact, the commercial executive gets the total variable income only in cases where they are able to give proof of the confidence they have built up with both old and new clients. A poor evaluation from clients or, even worse, their termination of an agreement with the bank, is interpreted as being down to the executive's lack of skill to inspire confidence. Indeed, as a young commercial executive points out: 'We have client campaigns where every day we have to call for their birthday. We also have relationship campaigns.' Failed sales suggest the executive's incompetence to detect clients' needs or to gain their confidence. In cases where a worker's sales rate or evaluation are poor, he or she is convened in private by the management and the situation is analysed.

In recent years, offices have been undergoing automation processes with the introduction of robots for client service and the computerisation of internal procedures and product sales. New branches reduce occupations such as cashier or client services (now automatic), internal process controllers (supplanted by software with some degree of deep learning), and executives devoted to simple financial operations (now replaced by web pages or mobile apps). On the other hand, there is an increase in the staff oriented to sales and interaction with clients. As previously mentioned, commercial executives lose their autonomy and control over the management of clients given the new business intelligence units which provide them with lists of potential consumers and their particular characteristics. This phenomenon involves a deskilling process because commercial executives – mostly women – lose control over their clients' portfolios and the ability to arrange their sales work autonomously. Likewise, computerised mechanisms of control in relation to office performance have arisen to boost competition within the bank. However, these new administrative control platforms are not a mystery for bank workers (Moore and Joyce 2020). In fact, new heads of the client-service platform are aware of the human work involved, mistakes in which can affect, for instance, the calculation of quarterly bonuses. In other cases, banking branches become a place where small and medium entrepreneurs can find an 'office' – known as a *workcafé* – and gain access to business networks, financial consultancy and funding for their projects: the executive is now a commercial adviser.

Figure 8.2 shows a strong reduction in the banking offices of the private banks (TLPB and RPB) since 2014. In fact, in only the last four years, the total number of banking offices fell by 239 at a national scale.[4] Currently, these are gradual changes which have not yet resulted in a massive process of automation; but they mark a trend that, in addition to the aforementioned qualitative changes, is transforming traditional offices into business environments for all kinds of entrepreneurs.

Telephone banking serves clients, files claims, and provides collection services and product sales. Workers in this area are low-skilled and

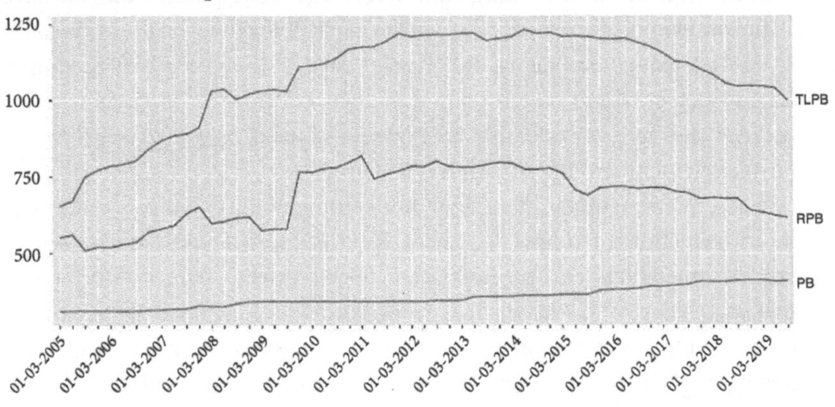

Figure 8.2 Banking Offices (2005–2019)
Source: Author's analysis based on SBIF data.

4. Headquarters, Branches, Auxiliary Boxes and Support Offices are considered.

mostly women, who master gendered skills such as listening, sympathy and telephone smiling (Crompton, Gallie and Purcell 2002). Indeed, as mentioned by a supervisor of this area, 'We still live in a sexist country. An important percentage of clients are men, so they feel better assisted by a woman.' In recent years, telephone banking has introduced automated reply devices (chatbots) and strengthened self-service mechanisms via digital platforms as a strategy for size and cost reduction (Jacobs et al. 2017).

In other cases, automated mechanisms of control have improved from traditional digital screens and traffic controllers (using colours for the management of work pace) to artificial intelligence software controlling in real time the tones and emotions used by executives to their clients – a sort of 'algorithmic control' (Wood et al. 2018) which is replacing direct human supervision in some banking processes. The placing of (human) telephone executives under new vigilance mechanisms is predominant in this labour process.

In sum, the introduction of new technologies in the banking labour process has developed two parallel dynamics of productive reorganisation (see Figure 8.3) – on the one hand, deskilling processes and greater control are boosting labour intensity; on the other hand, certain occupations or tasks are being directly replaced. All of which is triggered by a transformation in the banking industry where new financial services 'hold' an increasing added value from the combination of human labour and new technologies. However, the speed of implementation and the mistrust of some clients towards this interaction with new technologies have forced some measures to be either reversed or adjusted based on a more active participation of trade unions.

In any case, these changes in control mechanisms are triggering different types of resistance (both new and traditional), according to the labour process in which they are positioned. Headquarter and administrative offices present resistance towards the loss of autonomy (Friedman 1977) produced by the organisational changes, and skilled workers make direct complaints to the leadership. Claims arise in focus groups carried out by the bank when conflicts reach the higher hierarchy or pressure is applied through trade unions. What Movitz and Allvin (2017) show for the Swedish experience applies also in the Chilean case, namely that conflicts among management teams have emerged due to their leadership of organisational

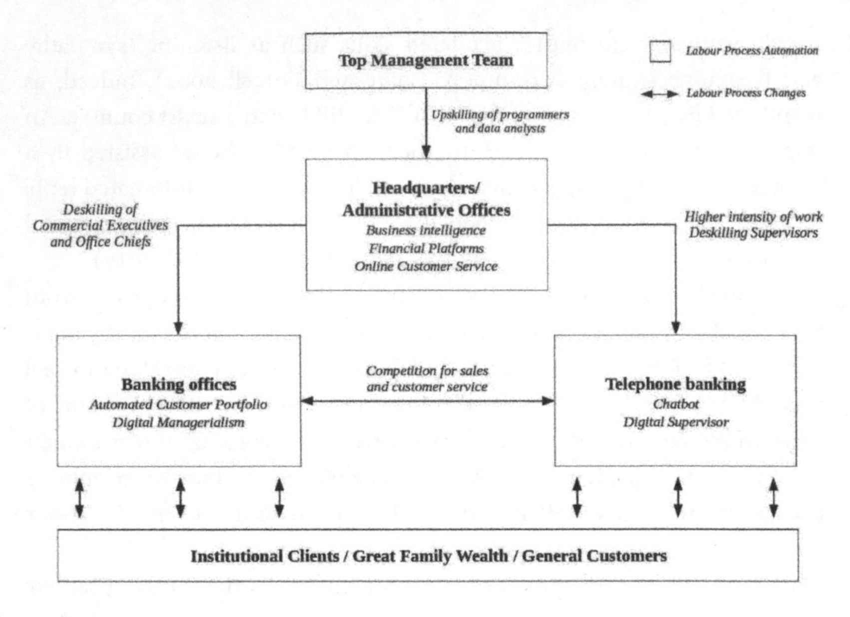

Figure 8.3 Organogram of Automation and Banking Labour Process
Source: Author's data.

changes related to the introduction of new technologies and the labour skills required for their implementation.

In banking offices, there are resistances to the boost of labour intensity produced by the automation process, to the constant change of bureaucratic rules defining the functions of each position, and to the growing salary flexibility – which has been translated into an increase of leadership and supervisors' unionisation. Negotiation efforts (Ackroyd and Thompson 1999) are exercised through the individual claim to the higher hierarchy or the collective claim in focus groups; the slow-down of processes for change implementation while developing parallel mechanisms to make a comparison with the productivity given by the computerised system; or appeals to the trade union in cases where negotiation agreements are infringed. Generally, the office chief makes an adjustment of the management criteria for the executives to be able to offer quality service; however, this is limited by the growth of demand for products. Along the same lines as Burawoy (1979), there is a formal and informal system of rules and penalties, encouragement of competition within an 'internal market', and a claim and collective negotiation system in which conflict can be converted into consent.

Finally, in telephone banking the main conflicts emerge as a result of changes introduced in the payments system, failures in the bank website, technical and direct mechanisms of control (Edwards 1979), and the lack of acknowledgement and holidays. Here, the main resistance methods range from job abandonment, sick leave attributed to work-related illness, arguments with supervisors, collective execution of poor evaluations, up to demands to the trade union. These struggles over the negotiation of labour quantity and intensity (Ackroyd and Thompson 1999; Woodcock 2017) have generated an increase of unionisation which has led to improvements in labour conditions.

In sum, automation of the banking labour process has triggered different resistances and higher levels of unionisation. However, not all resistances go against the greatest exploitation caused by these new forms of organisational and technological control. In particular, office heads and some skilled workers are reluctant to submit to pressure from the Top Management Team for the whole workforce to be oriented towards the sale of financial products. This resistance aims to ensure the quality of the service and, therefore, the stability of client confidence, which is not necessarily guaranteed by banking automation.

THE FUTURE OF THE BANKING LABOUR PROCESS

Automation is neither a linear nor an inevitable process. There are four main obstacles to a deeper and more widespread automation: first, the operational costs involved in its intensive introduction at productive and organisational levels and the relatively low cost of the female workforce which is currently employed; second, legal provisions regulating the banking industry, such as the obligatory employment of internal security guards; third, the resistance of some trade unions; fourth, the foundation the whole banking system is based on, namely, the reproduction of confidence relations between the institution and its clients.

One of the main boundaries in the deepening of this process is the automation of tasks and occupations directly related to human interaction, in particular those occupations oriented towards the inspiration of confidence between clients and the institution. This is due to different factors

– emotional skills that have not been easy to standardise; generational limitations in terms of clients who have a preference for traditional offices; security concerns around transactions; or the poor performance of modern virtual applications or organisational changes. But in any case, the evidence shows it is only a matter of time before fully-human services will be provided to large companies and wealthy families, while face-to-face interaction for other clients will be rationed according to their financial relevance for the bank.

Despite the dystopias foreshadowed in an unlaboured world, the most likely scenario is the replacement of traditional occupations by new ones, and a deskilling of traditional banking employees – especially commercial executives, cashiers, and general customer service and call centre workers. However, trade unions have so far complicated the acceleration of automation processes, and the space is still open for them to lead an agenda resisting the increase of labour intensity and encouraging upskilling or compensation for those affected by technological unemployment. The key issue is therefore not opposition to new technologies, but questioning the use to which they are being put in a capitalist production process that increases the exploitation of labour.

In conclusion, banking automation is not an ineluctable process, nor are its results determined a priori. As Marx pointed out in *Capital*, new technologies in capitalist production change forms of exploitation and organisation of the labour process. On the one hand, the expansion of a new labour force subordinated through platform control weakens traditional trade unions. On the other hand, since the extent and speed of labour deskilling affects both skilled and unskilled banking workers alike, they begin to resist and deploy new types of solidarity. The current transformations of the banking labour process could, then, open up opportunities for a new kind of unionism, at once more technological, flexible and feminist. The consequences of automation will thus mainly depend on whether trade unions can transform banking power relations to make these new technologies a powerful organisational instrument for achieving greater autonomy and welfare.

REFERENCES

Ackroyd, S. and Thompson, P. (1999). *Organizational Misbehaviour*. London: SAGE.

Boccardo, G. (2013). *Condiciones laborales en trabajadores del Sindicato Banco de Chile y Federación de Sindicatos del Banco de Chile*. Santiago: Ediciones Y Publicaciones El Buen Aire Sa.

Boccardo, G. (2019). Automatización de la banca chilena: transformación tecnológica y conflictos en el trabajo. *Revista Bits de Ciencia* 18. At www.dcc.uchile.cl/bits-de-ciencia.

Briken, K., Chillas, S. and Krzywdzinski, M. (2017). *The New Digital Workplace: How New Technologies Revolutionise Work*. Basingstoke: Palgrave Macmillan.

Brynjolfsson, E. and McAfee, A. (2014). *The Second Machine Age: Work, Progress, and Prosperity in a Time of Brilliant Technologies*. New York: W. W. Norton.

Burawoy, M. (1979). *Manufacturing Consent: Changes in the Labor Process Under Monopoly Capitalism*. Chicago: University of Chicago Press.

Crompton, R. (1989). Women in Banking: Continuity and Change Since the Second World War. *Work, Employment and Society* 3(2), 141–56.

Crompton, R., Gallie, D. and Purcell, K., eds. (2002). *Changing Forms of Employment: Organizations, Skills and Gender*. Abingdon: Routledge.

Edwards, R. (1979). *Contested Terrain*. New York: Basic Books.

Frías, P. (1990). *El trabajo bancario: liberalización, modernización y lucha por la democracia*. Santiago: Programa de Economía del Trabajo.

Friedman, A. (1977). Responsible Autonomy versus Direct Control Over the Labour Process. *Capital & Class* 1(1), 43–57.

Jacobs, I., Powers, S., Seguin, B. and Lynch, D. (2017). The Top 10 Chatbots for Enterprise Customer Service. *Forrester Report*. At www.nuance.com/content/dam/nuance/en_au/collateral/enterprise/report/ar-forrester-top10-chatbots-en-us.pdf.

Kalleberg, A. L. (2001). Organizing Flexibility: The Flexible Firm in a New Century. *British Journal of Industrial Relations* 39(4), 479–504.

Mauro, A. (2004). *Trayectorias laborales en el sector financiero. Recorrido de las mujeres*. Santiago: CEPAL.

Mella, O. and Parra, M. (1990). Condiciones de trabajo en el sector bancario chileno. In P. Frías, *El trabajo bancario: liberalización, modernización y lucha por la democracia*. Santiago: Programa de Economía del Trabajo.

Moore, P. and Joyce, S. (2020). Black Box or Hidden Abode? The Expansion and Exposure of Platform Work Managerialism. *Review of International Political Economy* 27(4), 926–48.

Moulian, T. (1997). *Chile actual: anatomía de un mito*. Santiago: Lom-ARCIS.

Movitz, F. and Allvin, M. (2017). Changing Systems, Creating Conflicts: IT-related Changes in Swedish Banking. In K. Briken et al., eds. *The New Digital Workplace: How New Technologies Revolutionise Work*. Basingstoke: Palgrave Macmillan, 132–52.

Narbona, K. (2012). *La producción de compromiso en la empresa flexible. Significados que los trabajadores dan al compromiso subjetivo con el trabajo, ante las nuevas técnicas de gestión de recursos humanos. Estudio de caso de un banco multinacional en Santiago de Chile* (Thesis). Universidad de Chile, Santiago, Chile.

Riquelme, V. (2013). *Actuaciones y políticas de género en empresas del sector bancario. Departamento de Estudios de la Dirección del Trabajo*. Santiago: Departamento de Estudios, Dirección del Trabajo.

Ruiz, C. and Boccardo, G. (2014). *Los chilenos bajo el neoliberalismo. Clases y conflicto social.* Santiago: El Desconcierto.

Sadovska, K. and Kamola, L. (2017). Change Management in Operations in the Banking Sector During the 4th Industrial Revolution. In *Contemporary Challenges in Management and Economics*. Riga: Riga Technical University, 43–6.

Sathye, M. (1999). Adoption of Internet Banking by Australian Consumers: An Empirical Investigation. *International Journal of Bank Marketing* 17(7), 324–34.

Srnicek, N. and Williams, A. (2015). *Inventing the Future: Postcapitalism and a World Without Work*. London: Verso.

Thompson, P., Warhurst, C. and Callaghan, G. (2001). Ignorant Theory and Knowledgeable Workers: Interrogating the Connections Between Knowledge, Skills and Services. *Journal of Management Studies* 38(7), 923–42.

Wood, A. J., Graham, M., Lehdonvirta, V. and Hjorth, I. (2018). Good Gig, Bad Gig: Autonomy and Algorithmic Control in the Global Gig Economy. *Work, Employment and Society* 33(1), 56–75.

Woodcock, J. (2017). *Working the Phones: Control and Resistance in Call Centres*. London: Pluto.

PART III

Breaking It

9
It Gets Better With Age: AI and the Labour Process in Old and New Gig-Economy Firms

Adam Badger

CONTEXTUALISING TECHNOLOGY AND COURIER WORK

Emerging out of the shift towards postindustrial capitalism, courier work has always had a symbiotic relationship with technology and the city, its fate hanging precariously in the balance between technological 'progress', markets and the demand for daredevil workers willing to take on traffic-filled streets. The industry's heyday predates the ubiquity of the fax machine, scanning technologies and ultimately email as the only fast and reliable method of transporting documents and packages across urban space. This speed was afforded by removing the central 'distribution centre' – required for national delivery networks such as the Royal Mail and FedEx – instead favouring an agile fleet of dispersed couriers able to pick up and drop off packages direct from door-to-door. Here, it is a human 'controller' that receives calls from clients and dispatches them to messengers, harnessing the personal and collective intimate knowledges of the city and their workforce in order to do so.

While the gap between the market's need for documents to move quickly and technological infrastructures capable of doing so carved out a lucrative niche for couriers to work in, it was their adoption of analogue communication technologies that allowed this to function. Early pioneers of the New York courier scene would set out for the day with a pocket full of quarters, using pay-phones to call back to 'base' and pick up another series of jobs, memorising the details in their heads or jotting them down on slips of paper as they went. Next came the introduction of CB Radio, as masts and equipment became cheap enough for firms to achieve full city coverage, greatly reducing the communicative friction of dispatching work. Finally, in a shift towards the digital, some firms began using PDAs and mobile applications to organise their nomadic messenger fleets (for further background, see Day 2015; Kidder 2011). While CB Radio remains a staple for a dwindling number of traditional firms, a new breed of 'gig-economy' services have entered the market with app-based platforms, in turn replacing the 'controller' with assemblages of machine learning software and algorithms in an effort to increase speed, order volume and so-called 'efficiency'. The distributed human 'intelligences' of the work (of controllers who manage fleets, and of couriers' intimate knowledge of the city) are being replaced by algorithmic intelligences, backed by investment capital that seeks to standardise and routinise this work.

Rather than growing and adopting technologies over time, gig platforms have entered the market with the promise of new technological tools as their USP (Unique Selling Point). By branding themselves as 'disruptors' they attempt to veil their own refinements to organisational technologies in addition to any claims workers or regulators may have on restraining their behaviour. However, patterns in their growth are beginning to emerge. Efforts to self-position as mavericks, unrestrained by any previous way of doing things, are starting to give way under the weight of evidence accumulating against them. In this chapter, I argue that gig-economy courier firms are in fact far more homogeneous in their approach than first meets the eye, following a similar progression as those that have gone before. While differences in the finer details of the work may give riders the opportunity to game the system as much as possible, these firms ultimately follow a shared path and destiny, marching to the beat of the shareholder's drum.

THE CONCEPTUAL AI: DO SHAREHOLDERS DREAM OF ELECTRIC STREETS?

To reveal the shareholder presence in the gig economy's labour organisation and the development of AI technologies, we need to go back in time to 2008. Following the financial crash, platforms were heralded as a silver bullet to solve the employment and financial crisis. The unemployed could once again sign up in the morning and be out working in the afternoon. Simultaneously, the Janus-like spectre of platform capitalism (Srnicek 2017) provided an avenue for all the stagnant cash floating around in the economy to find an escape. Interest rates were negligibly above zero, and inflation was devaluing the savings of investment funds, pension funds and ultra-high-net-worth individuals alike. Blue-chip stock prices had stalled, and the mortgage/property market was in a downward spiral. However, by buying-in early, and building diverse investment portfolios, huge financial returns were promised in exchange for getting behind the hyped-up Silicon Valley and Roundabout firms like Uber and Deliveroo that were just debuting in the global marketplace and consciousness.

At the centre of these firms' promise to shareholders was a move away from the piece-rate jobs of the past, and into a new era of technologically divined efficiencies that would – once fully developed – garner massive returns on investment as the costs of matching supply and demand, as well as the provision of service, became negligible. Rather inconveniently, however, complex algorithmic assemblages capable of engineering these efficiencies cannot simply be 'made up' out of the ether. These systems are built over time, in collaboration with enormous datasets. As such, the promise of speculative advances in AI technologies become married to the speculative financial models that encourage investment in the gig economy. While some technology companies have been able to outsource this data production via micro-working platforms (see for example, Casilli 2019; Tubaro and Casilli 2019), this is inappropriate for cycle courier firms. The geographically 'sticky' nature of service delivery (see Woodcock and Graham 2020) – i.e. that it happens *in* place – means that the highly contextualised data needed to create efficiencies must come from interactions that happen in urban space. The challenge for platforms, then, is to find a way to capture highly detailed datasets, calibrated to the context in which they are being applied, that can then be 'fed' to machine learning algorithms for the divination of efficiencies in the labour process. If these efficiencies aren't achieved, then the company will struggle to reach profitability, investor confidence will falter and, with it, the company's valuation.

These technologically enabled promises can be seen most clearly in the investor pitch decks that platforms give to venture capitalists in the early stages, which are sadly not publicly available. However, we can see the ongoing impact of these promises in the filings gig-economy companies have made when moving towards an Initial Public Offering (IPO). These documents are written to outline the potential risks and opportunities to investors by exploring corporate strategy. These secretive companies must reluctantly make public their aims and aspirations in order to avoid the risk of later charges of fraud from regulators such as the Securities and Exchange Commission (SEC). For example, in their IPO documents, Uber stated that:

> Managing the complexity of our massive network and harnessing the data from over 10 billion trips exceeds human capability, so we use machine learning and artificial intelligence, trained on historical transactions, to help automate marketplace decisions. We have built a machine learning software platform that powers hundreds of models behind our data-driven services across our offerings and in customer service and safety ... [as a result] Our network becomes smarter with every trip. (Uber 2019: 146; 155–6).

The notion of a growing network intelligence, rooted in the 'trips' that take place across urban space, clearly highlights the way in which start-up and shareholder imaginaries coalesce around the idea of AI: that by developing/investing early and providing the expertise/capital to advance these intelligent systems, start-ups/shareholders can make massive returns and be at the forefront of some of the most 'innovative' companies of our time, reshaping whole economies in their favour. The part that is left out of this equation however, is the workers, whose bodies and smartphones become surfaces of translation from vast urban environments to zeros and ones that can be computed and iterated by ever more intelligent machine learning systems.

PATTERNS OF DEVELOPMENT

As this chapter turns towards workers and the experience of work, it is necessary to pause over the empirical basis for these developments. This research is the result of nine months of covert ethnographic fieldwork, during which I worked for two delivery platforms in London's gig economy. This is paired with semi-structured interviews with other workers, and 18 months of overt ethnographic fieldwork with the trade union responsible for organising their respective workforces. The platforms in question have been given pseudonyms, in line with my ethical review agreement with my college – a critical discussion of which can be found elsewhere (Badger and Woodcock 2019). They have been given the names Mercury Meals and Iris

Delivery.[1] Mercury Meals is a B2C market leader in London's food-delivery scene, and is currently still in the venture stages of funding. It operates across a range of Eurasian markets. Iris Delivery's B2B platform has now been acquired by another larger operator, but continues to transport both takeaway meals and other packages under its brand across the capital. Beyond London, it operates across a range of European cities.

While the companies in question have developed their own idiosyncratic labour-processes, market niches and workforces, there have been similar patterns of development across both platforms. Mercury Meals was founded two years prior to Iris Delivery, and has enjoyed significantly greater cash injections. As such, they are considerably more advanced than Iris, whose diminished market share means that less trips have been made, and, as such, the network is not as 'smart'. These patterns and differences are reflected on below, before moving on to a discussion of how workers may utilise the differences between the two in their attempts to carve out a living in this under-paid, highly precarious work.

DATA GENERATION

In the case of traditional cycle courier work, contact between human couriers and human dispatchers is kept to a minimum. However, in the case of the gig economy, this is transformed into a high-touch relationship (see McDowell 2009 for more on high-touch service work) as riders are expected to report their progress through interaction with the platform via the worker app. While riders can undertake any job however they like through their own choice of route, they are forced to engage with the technological interface, creating a trail of data in the process.

This leads me to follow Moore and Joyce, who challenge 'the uncritical black box approach' which they argue 'does not go far enough to expose intentionality in management practices' (2020: 15) – something that Van Doorn and Badger (2020) also build on to reveal how the expropriation of workers' data represents the hidden abode of platform capitalism. This occurs

1. These names were chosen after mythological figures tasked with delivery or couriering. Mercury is the Roman courier god of communication, in addition to presiding over financial gain, commerce, luck, trickery and thieves. Iris is a Greek messenger god, also responsible for the weather. I hope the irony in these gods' para-delivery duties can be appreciated. Any associations are fully intended.

through the hard-wiring of data-capture practice into labour processes. This represents an additional labour process, overlaid onto that of the physical delivery, whereby couriers are forced into data creation. At Mercury Meals, for example, couriers are expected to notify the platform via an app on their smartphone each time they 1) accept an order, 2) arrive at the restaurant, 3) pick up the food, 4) arrive at the customer's address, and 5) drop off the food and complete the order. This input punctuates the backdrop of continuous geolocation, with data events that feed the platform's management algorithm. Furthermore, it is required for the courier to be able to access the next stage of the job (i.e. workers cannot know the customer's delivery address until they have digitally notified the platform that they have picked up the package). By building a labour process that gradually unwinds this information asymmetry in stages that respond to input, workers are coerced into the process, regardless of the professed 'freedoms' that come with the job. Critically though, it generates highly granular data about the individualised progress of a given job, which, when aggregated with that of other couriers, becomes parseable by Mercury Meals' or Iris Delivery's machine learning algorithms for the generation of further efficiencies in the future. In short, to carry out their work today, workers are forced to create data that will go on to be part of the broader 'efficiency making' of tomorrow.

These platforms' insatiable appetite for data highlights the significance it holds for their business model (and for the promises made to shareholders about efficiencies that were outlined above). As such, workers enter into a process of dual value production whereby they are exploited for the labour of their delivery, while their data labour is expropriated at the moment of production. The insights from these datasets only end up creating efficiencies that diminish the unit cost of labour provision and therefore the pay packets of couriers. Worse still, *every* interaction with the platform becomes a site of data generation. Initially, justification was not needed for the rejection of a job; however, over time, justifications have been added in the form of multiple-choice lists that riders can choose from (such as 'mechanical breakdown', or 'pick-up distance too far'). This renders even the act of work refusal as quantified data, parseable for further efficiencies in the platforms' attempt to reduce job rejection.

Both Mercury and Iris have tweaked their approach to data labour taking place on their platforms over time as they become more developed. The difference between the younger and the older company here is the sophistication of data capture, and its granularity. As systems become more developed, they require ever more granular and contextualised data to continue returning results, which is mirrored in the process of the data's creation (see Gitelman 2013).

FROM INDIVIDUAL MANAGEMENT TO FLEET MANAGEMENT

While traditional courier firms harness human capabilities in their fleet management, gig platforms in the early stages of their development were incapable of managing in such a holistic manner. Instead, each job and each worker were managed individually by dispatch algorithms. This meant that jobs were given to the rider who was closest to the pick-up location and that once a job was completed riders were expected to return to a common meeting place, colloquially known as a 'zone centre', strategically located near the most popular pick-up locations. While this sounds sensible, it is an acutely inefficient way of doing business. Couriers end up covering vast 'dead-miles'[2] in their work and are thus being 'unproductive'. Instead of journeys going from A-B-C-D, this approach takes riders from A-B-A-C-A-D, wherein all the trips returning to 'A' are unpaid. This is bad for the couriers, who experience a reduced earning potential, and bad for the platform, as job completion is slower and reduced earnings lead to resistance efforts among workers.

Mercury Meals was the first to move into fleet management, as they integrated their various datasets into the 'intelligent' dispatch algorithm's stack. A new version of the platform's central algorithm promised that jobs would no longer be served to the closest rider, and instead would be issued based on a range of factors including 'the specific item being prepared, and the amount of time it will take; the location of the pick-up point; the number of couriers also logged-on and working; the time of day and week; how many other live orders there are; and the distance from pick-up location to drop-off location'.[3] This follows the lead of already established courier firms, whose human controllers bring together 'routes' for workers that consist of multiple jobs, keeping their bag full at all times, and meaning they are

2. Dead miles refer to distances covered without any jobs on-board. These are seen as a massive waste in courier circles, and the aim is to reduce them as much as possible.
3. Note, this has been paraphrased to protect Mercury Meals' identity. Copying directly from their public facing material would have left their identity only a cursory Google search away.

making more money, more efficiently (see also Chappell 2016; Day 2015; Sayarer 2016).

While this meant riders would, in theory, receive more work and therefore more pay, it actually obfuscated the technological decision-making process involved in the assignment of work. Those who had worked for the platform the longest therefore lost their edge in the marketplace, as the experience they had developed of working in collaboration with Mercury Meals' AI was rendered useless overnight. Now, waiting in strategically beneficial locations, near to the quickest restaurants, was pointless, as orders were assigned based on more numerous factors. Similarly, the algorithm prioritised certain riders during certain times and conditions, without any explanation or justification as for why. While the efficiency of the platform as a whole increased, the amount of agency workers had over their own labour process was strictly limited.

This development took place at Mercury Meals prior to my research commencing. However myself and other workers were under the impression that Iris Delivery began testing this change during my fieldwork. The impact was palpable, as we felt the platform change from slow and stable to capricious and unpredictable. One participant noted at interview that they felt they had gone from a sense of security to now 'trying to please the algorithm gods all the time' to make enough money to survive. These, sadly, are the human costs of the data-derived efficiencies promised to shareholders. While in traditional courier firms dispatchers often come from the industry and share a personal knowledge of the frustrations slow work brings, the white-collar programmers, ordered to code shareholder logics and desires into the technological infrastructure, share no such common knowledge or sense of solidarity. The very human problem of feeling precarious at work and hoping for a stable income is rendered as a mathematical challenge to be solved in the move towards a theoretically improved fleet system.

MULTI-APPING

In order to survive, workers needed to respond. One strategy is to down tools and take to the streets to protest – a strategy I fully advocate, and which is explored elsewhere by other writers (Cant 2018, 2020; Woodcock 2020). However, due to the constraints of the chapter, I will focus here on strategies developed at work.

With platform technologies becoming less predictable in their job distribution methods, workers are left in need of increasing their chances of being offered work. Given the heavy focus on take-away deliveries, workers are already under considerable pressure to compress a day's earnings into a short space of 'peak' time (either the lunchtime or dinnertime rush). Experienced couriers who once knew the best places to wait to take advantage of these surges in demand needed to reassess their approach. By signing up to two different platforms and logging in simultaneously, workers are able (in theory) to double their chances of being offered work. This is known colloquially as 'multi-apping' and is a phenomenon that has seen massive growth following these technological changes.

While heavily frowned upon by both platforms in question, multi-apping is only made possible by their insistence on classifying workers as 'independent contractors'. Although this is widely perceived as an attempt to shirk the responsibilities they owe couriers (such as holiday and sick pay), it does open up the possibility of working for multiple platforms at once (see Cherry and Aloisi 2017, for example). Furthermore, multi-apping relies on the overlap of spatial coverage by each platform. This is easier in large, dense markets such as London, but less so in smaller towns that might only be serviced by one platform. During my time working for Iris and Mercury, I provided services in the busy East Central area of London – stretching from Whitechapel to St Pauls, and from Aldgate to Hackney.

It should be noted that multi-apping isn't an ideal situation, or seen as a 'positive' opportunity for entrepreneurial behaviour; rather it is most often deployed as a survival strategy as labour conditions worsen. To survive, workers must internalise the differences between each platform's technologically mediated rhythms of work. Mercury Meals, for example, had a higher frequency of jobs during peak times, that were often less well paid, but very short distance. Iris meanwhile paid more per job, but most jobs required longer wait and travel times than the offerings available at Mercury. Outside of peak times, Iris's market diversity beyond food delivery meant there was a slow trickle of work available, while for Mercury there was relatively little. As such, workers who are well versed in the differences can harness both platforms in their attempts to make a living, choosing times and locations in which to supply their labour, and carefully curating the jobs they take to ensure they maximise their profit potential.

The risk of not internalising these technologies well enough is the poor or misjudged performance of work, and subsequent 'termination'. The consequence of the elaborate capture apparatus developed by platforms to derive data and subsequent efficiency is a landscape of oligoptic surveillance playing out through an assemblage of digital and urban space. While workers are free in some elements of their work – and can evade a platform's surveillance efforts by simply logging off – the sophisticated technologies that now rest at the heart of advanced gig-economy firms have been granted the authority to make automated decisions. Get caught doing something the computational framework deems wrong, and you risk being fired with immediate effect. As the systems get more intelligent with every trip taken, workers must become more nuanced in their approaches to making a living in the platform economy.

CONCLUSION

It is clear that combining huge datasets with machine learning technologies in the hope of divining efficiency is shaping the platform economy and the experience of work within it. As critical scholars, it is essential we disregard the notion that technology is somehow 'objective' and devoid of external influence. The assemblage of management algorithms at the heart of the two companies discussed are as they are for a reason. The logics of platform capitalism are hard-coded into them and the labour processes they arbitrate, creating a particular kind of efficiency gain that favours only one side of the equation. As such, platforms have become the conduits for shareholder logics, providing yet another avenue for capital to grow as the direct result of exploited labour. Worse still, in this model, workers are not only exploited for their physical labour of food delivery, but have their data expropriated at the point of production in a process Harvey (2005) has called accumulation by dispossession. Following Fraser (2016: 165), focusing exclusively on 'capital's exploitation of wage labor in commodity production' (i.e. on only the physical labour of the work) marginalises the entangled process of (data) expropriation that operates as its condition of possibility. As such, advances in AI and the promise of an infinite future of efficiency gains are being sold to shareholders by platforms who become complicit in recreating their logics of exponential growth and cost/risk management.

This is only made possible through the transformation of work from a low-touch, autonomous occupation into the high-touch activity it has become. Each touch creates data, and, with enough data and computing power, 'efficiencies' create cost reductions. Those who reduce enough and attain a monopoly position through aggressive growth can be rewarded with enormous profits and dividends. This is no clearer than in Deliveroo's reporting of 107,117 per cent growth over the four years from 2014–18 (Deloitte 2018), alongside a bumper remuneration for their founder and CEO Will Shu, who last year paid himself £250,000 and received £8.3 million in share options. Meanwhile, in my time at the trade union that organises its workers, I frequently interfaced with riders working 60+ hours a week and still facing the fear of eviction. This perspective is sadly confirmed by Field and Forsey's parliamentary report that found riders' average earnings tended 'to hover a little above, a little below, or at the level of the National Living Wage', while some reported being 'on £1.60 or less an hour at times' (2018: 17). Out of necessity and ingenuity, workers show great skill and knowledge in finding ways to cut through this difficult landscape. Ultimately however, while the platforms do indeed 'get smarter with every trip', riders are not able to enjoy this same luxury. Yes, experience helps, but rapid changes to distribution technologies and rates of pay can render them useless overnight. Machine learning technologies are central to this inequality and existential sense of precarity. Future research should address ways of improving this balance.

REFERENCES

Badger, A. and Woodcock, J. (2019). Ethnographic Methods with Limited Access: Assessing Quality of Work in Hard to Reach Jobs. In D. Wheatley, ed. *Handbook of Research Methods on the Quality of Working Lives*. Cheltenham: Edward Elgar, 135–46.

Cant, C. (2018). The Wave of Worker Resistance in European Food Platforms 2016–17. *Notes From Below*. At https://notesfrombelow.org/article/european-food-platform-strike-wave.

Cant, C. (2020). *Riding for Deliveroo: Resistance in the New Economy.* Cambridge: Polity.

Casilli, A. (2019). *En attendant les robots. Enquête sur le travail du clic* [Waiting for the Robots: An Inquiry into Clickwork]. Paris: Editions du Seuil.

Chappell, E. (2016). *What Goes Around: A London Cycle Courier's Story*. London: Guardian/ Faber & Faber.

Cherry, M. A. and Aloisi, A. (2017). 'Dependent Contractors' in the Gig Economy: A Comparative Approach. *American University Law Review* 66(3), 635–89.

Day, J. (2015). *Cyclogeography: Journeys of A London Bicycle Courier*. London: Notting Hill Editions.

Deloitte (2018). Fast50 Winner: Deliveroo. At www.deloitte.co.uk/fast50/winners/2018/winner-profiles/deliveroo.

Field, F. and Forsey, A. (2018). *Delivering Justice? A Report on the Pay and Working Conditions of Deliveroo Riders*. Commissioned by Frank Field, MP. Prepared for the Work and Pensions Committee. At www.frankfield.co.uk/upload/docs/Delivering%20justice.pdf.

Fraser, N. (2016). Expropriation and Exploitation in Racialized Capitalism: A Reply to Michael Dawson. *Critical Historical Studies* 3(1), 163–78.

Gitelman, L. (2013). *There's No Such Thing as Raw Data*. Cambridge, MA: MIT Press.

Harvey, D. (2005). *The New Imperialism*. Oxford: Oxford University Press.

Kidder, J. (2011). *Urban Flow: Bike Messengers and the City*. New York: Cornell University Press.

McDowell, L. (2009). *Working Bodies: Interactive Service Employment and Workplace Identities*. London: Wiley-Blackwell.

Moore, P. and Joyce, S. (2020) 'Black Box or Hidden Abode? The Expansion and Exposure of Platform Work Managerialism'. Special Issue 'The Political Economy of Management', eds. Samuel Knafo and Matthew Eagleton-Pierce. *Review of International Political Economy* 27(3).

Sayarer, J. (2016). *Messengers: City Tales from a London Courier*. London: Arcadia Books.

Srnicek, N. (2017). *Platform Capitalism*. Cambridge: Polity.

Tubaro, P. and Casilli, A. (2019). Micro-work, Artificial Intelligence and the Automotive Industry. *Journal of Industrial and Business Economics* 46, 333–45.

Uber Technologies, Inc. (2019). Registration Statement under the Securities Act of 1933. At www.sec.gov/Archives/edgar/data/1543151/000119312519103850/d647752ds1.htm.

Van Doorn, N. and Badger, A. (2020). Platform Capitalism's Hidden Abode: Producing Data Assets in the Gig Economy. *Antipode*. At https://doi.org/10.1111/anti.12641.

Woodcock, J. (2020). The Algorithmic Panopticon at Deliveroo: Measurement, Precarity, and the Illusion of Control. *Ephemera*. At www.ephemerajournal.org/contribution/algorithmic-panopticon-deliveroo-measurement-precarity-and-illusion-control.

Woodcock, J. and Graham, M. (2020). *The Gig Economy: A Critical Introduction*. Cambridge: Polity.

10
Self-Tracking and Sousveillance at Work: Insights from Human-Computer Interaction and Social Science

Marta E. Cecchinato, Sandy J. J. Gould and Frederick Harry Pitts

In this chapter we consider whether and how new collective practices of shared aggregation and curation of individual data stand to enrich our understanding of the physical and emotional impacts of work and undergird coordinated responses to contemporary societal and industrial challenges around well-being and productivity in the workplace and beyond. Specifically, we are interested in whether there is something potentially emancipatory in these individualised and individualising routines and practices of self-quantification. Can workplace AI, algorithmic measurement and control and other tools for self-quantification be repurposed and wielded in support of collective resistance?

Under the post-war settlement, the industrial concord between workers and employers allowed the former to bargain with the latter over productivity compromises based on a quantitative understanding of the work, time and effort achievable due to the standardised character of the labour that took place in large, unionised industries and the standardised systems of measurement that followed. The contemporary political economy of the UK, meanwhile, is characterised by a very different set of circumstances: deindustrialisation and the rise of the service sector, the decline of trade unions and the destandardisation of employment relations towards a proliferation of precarious working patterns. All these contribute to work regimes that seemingly render unreproducible the kinds of measurement – typified in bits rolling off a production line in a given period of time – upon which workers once bargained for better.

At the same time, however, the use of distributed technologies of data capture and analysis increasingly characterise the changing world of work. In diverse contexts – the platform economy, warehousing and logistics, the hybrid spaces of creative and freelance work – individual behaviour is measured, monitored and predicted by sensors, apps and algorithms. Whether as a tool of managerial control or as a means of ensuring personal productivity and well-being, this 'quantification of the self' is both socially individualised and performatively individualising. Management deploy wearable tech and other means of data capture to identify sub-optimal individual performance among the workforce. At the same time, individuals themselves use the same or similar tech to develop more productive working practices inside and outside the workplace.

As we will see, there is always a collective dimension to the individualised subjectivity that self-quantification projects. Moreover, there is also a potential for new collective practices of shared aggregation and curation of individual data that enrich our understanding of work and hold the possibility of undergirding coordinated responses to contemporary societal and industrial challenges around well-being and productivity in the workplace and beyond. There is potential, we propose, not only for a greater understanding of the physical and affective impacts of contemporary work, but for a framework of bargaining over the terms under which that work is performed and remunerated in a world where clear measures and values of one's work and its worth are increasingly abstract and out of reach. Specifically, we suggest, this centres on a form of 'sousveillance', which we understand here as an inversion of surveillance, in other words the monitoring of management practices by and for workers rather than the other way around.

In this chapter these issues are explored by means of a literature review examining the intersections, and potential gaps, between the fields of sociology and Human-Computer Interaction (HCI) on the use of self-quantification technologies in the workplace, and their potential to be used by employees for collective resistance against workplace exploitation. The structure of the chapter is as follows. First, we chart some of the key themes of relevance in the literature on self-tracking. Second, we look at how practices of surveillance and sousveillance are addressed across the social sciences and the field of HCI. Third, we look specifically at workplace applications of both self-tracking and sousveillance. Finally, we explore both individual and collective representations and practices of self-tracking as a form of resistance in and beyond the workplace.

PERSONAL INFORMATICS AND SELF-TRACKING

In HCI, self-tracking is often understood as a form of personal informatics, a class of systems that help people collect and reflect on personal information to improve self-knowledge (Li et al. 2010). Personal informatics models have been developed because such systems are believed to help one change one's behaviour, with the most common benefit among users perceived to be 'consciousness raising' (Kersten van-Dijk et al. 2016). A key theme of HCI research on personal informatics is how designers use the representation of data to engage and influence people in processes of tracking and reflection. Data is usually selected and represented in a way that, designers hope, will allow people to reflect and so generate insight into their behaviour.

Because of this aesthetic and speculative dimension to data, several researchers have been investigating alternative ways of representing and visualising personal informatics data and its impact upon how users remember and reflect (Whooley et al. 2014; Epstein et al. 2014; Khot et al. 2014; Elsden et al. 2016). The embodied experience of users interacting with their own data is also an important strand within this field of research (Gardner and Jenkins 2015). Increasingly the use of such technologies is 'enmeshed' in everyday lived experience such that 'lived informatics' encapsulate lapses in, and even the abandonment of, tracking (Epstein et al. 2015; Rooksby 2014). In particular, the 'Quantified Self' movement based on 'self-knowledge through numbers' has led to many commercial self-tracking technologies aimed at everything from eating to physical activity and health-related issues.

It is important to note here that these definitions and models often assume that ownership and agency over data collection belong to the user, whose data is being tracked. However, personal informatics can include tracked data about any individual, not just one's 'self' (Li et al. 2010). This has been a key theme of social science engagement with the topic and with the HCI research around it. The move towards 'self-management', 'responsibilisation' of the individual, or a 'control society' is a key theme addressed in this literature (Lupton 2016; Moore and Robinson 2015; and Neff and Nafus 2016). Lupton, for example, identifies a gap in the existing HCI literature on self-tracking insofar as 'in their focus on the individual they do not explain the wider dimensions of the practice [of] "self-tracking cultures"' (Lupton 2014: 78). According to Lupton, 'this juxtaposition of the personal with the sociocultural aspects of computer informatics has yet to be fully explored and articulated in relation to self-tracking' (Lupton 2014: 78). The bringing to bear of sociological perspectives, therefore, may help in identifying the more collective processes and potentialities latent in what appears as an individualising and individualised set of technologies and uses.

WORKPLACE APPLICATIONS

HCI papers often focus in detail on the design of a specific app or device, reviewing user experience and creating recommendations for improving design; for instance, reviewing the boundary management issues created by smartphone email use and recommending improvements to email apps to help users maintain a healthy work-life balance (Cecchinato et al. 2014; 2015). HCI research of this kind has been particularly innovative and design-focused, even prototyping a Quantified Workplace system to gather various data and survey what employees found useful, providing design recommendations for future systems (Mathur et al. 2015).

There have also been attempts to understand how companies use tracking technology in the workplace to monitor worker performance or fatigue, capture mood and interpersonal influence or emotional awareness, correct sedentary behaviours, augment physical or cognitive processes, track movement or steps, evaluate time management and work breaks, identify individual workers, or deliver messages or other content to workers (Maman et al. 2017; Hänsel 2016; Moore and Robinson 2015). Specific case studies have focused on construction, occupational health (Schall et al. 2018), the police (Eneman et al. 2018), warehousing and logistics (Moore 2019), Amazon Mechanical Turk (Lascau et al. 2019) and assembly lines at Foxconn and Olivetti (Moore and Robinson 2015).

A specific area in which such an inquiry has been taken up in both social sciences and HCI is around the topic of time or 'rhythm' as a feature of self-tracking practices (Pitts et al. 2020; Iqbal et al. 2014). In a recent contribution, Davies (2019) looks at the desire to control rhythm – of both work and bodies – which is facilitated by wearable devices and real-time data. This attention to time often throws up a similarity between self-tracking in the workplace today and the forms of measurement and control through which workers were tracked in the Taylorist factory. Daechong (2017) uses speculative future scenarios to look at how the 'expected self-empowerment and self-improvement of users [is] rewritten as a "digital nudge", "extreme Taylorism", and "intimate surveillance" in [digital healthcare and labour management] settings.' Moore (2018a, b), meanwhile, traces a line between Taylor and the Gilbreths' 'Scientific Method', where management attempted to find a single perfect way to do work and standardise all work, and the Quantified Workplace, where individual workers self-manage using data as a tool to improve their own productivity.

Moore's work in particular marks a substantial contribution to the critical social-scientific understanding of the implications of self-tracking for the practice and experience of work. Specifically, she highlights how the pressure to self-manage and self-track is an outcome of the precarious conditions (zero-hours contracts, uncertain work futures), and expectations of agility (adaptability to constant change) imposed upon contemporary workers, the result of which is a commodification of emotional and affective labour (Moore 2018b; Moore and Piwek 2017). Examples covered in Moore's research include both voluntary self-monitoring, as in a Dutch company who took part in a Quantified Workplace experiment (Moore 2019), and technological tracking enforced by management in various contexts, for instance in large corporations such as Tesco (Moore and Robinson 2015). This kind of top-down tracking and algorithmic control is also common in new platform-based work (Wood et al. 2019).

POWER AND CONTROL IN TRACKING

Noting the tendency for work to blur into leisure time due to an 'always online' culture (Cecchinato et al. 2017), HCI research uses the term 'boundary management' to describe the problem of maintaining work-life balance and setting appropriate boundaries to tracking. This is imperative when the use of personal informatics at work brings into the domain of workplace measure issues typically considered outside the scope of the employment relationship, like health, sleep and mood – an accounting process that Moore describes as 'wellbilling' (Moore 2019: 137). In light of this, both social science and HCI literature identify user privacy at work as a key concern, highlighting the importance of transparency over data usage and usage permissions (Mathur et al. 2015; Moore and Piwek 2017; Schall et al. 2018).

Where does the locus of control lie in the collection of tracked data, the analyses performed and the decisions being made about it? For some scholars, the trend for self-tracking feeds into existing fears around increased everyday surveillance. The relationship between self-tracking and the wider role of data in contemporary capitalism rests upon an ownership and commodification structure whereby data is not privately available to the individual; most devices require uploading information to a cloud-based service, allowing corporations to benefit from either personal or anonymised datasets, and leaving the individual with little control over their data. In a work context, managers may have access to data which individuals cannot see (or may not know is being collected), and it may be unclear how data is being used to assess performance. In this sense, the social scientific and HCI scholarship on self-quantification takes a critical perspective based on self-tracking's position within a wider political economy of data that infringes upon the privacy and freedom of individuals in a number of ways and establishes limits on the potential of self-tracking for social good.

From this critical perspective, data collection only represents the individual within their existing conditions within the social relations to which they are currently subject at work and in everyday life. Where self-tracking seeks to capture productivity, health and well-being impacts, the onus falls on the individual to enact change based on the data they gather, to enhance their productivity or desirability and gain advantage, applying an individualised and competitive mindset to both their personal and professional life. Moreover, the data is not situated within a group or local context in such a way as to place responsibility on any powerful agencies to create wider change.

There are other ways of harnessing tracking data, though. Sousveillance is the idea that tracking can provide 'watchful vigilance from underneath' (Mann 2002) rather than just providing a way for firms and the state to monitor behaviour. The small body of work on the potential for tracking to hold power to account through sousveillance tends to focus on isolated instances rather than the broader principle, with cases including police body cameras (Eneman et al. 2018), healthcare technologies (Morgan 2014) and supervision and ethics in nursing (Freshwater et al. 2013). Few of these directly address work, workers or the workplace as a specific focus for the implementation of or experimentation with techniques of sousveillance. One example of work-focused sousveillance is Turkopticon (Irani and Silberman 2013), where workers on Amazon Mechanical Turk – a crowdsourcing gig platform – collaborate to report on employers. This involves simple ratings of employers: collective selection, curation and aggregation of individual measures are not features of the tool.

Sousveillance is necessarily a shared endeavour. Large monolithic actors like corporations and governments have the capacity to aggregate data at scale. Individuals can only achieve similar scale by pooling their data. Users and designers alone face limits to the extent of the changes they can achieve to how self-tracking technologies are deployed. It is necessary for 'self-tracking communities [to] form coalitions with other peer production-oriented groups, open source developers, crowdfunding communities and scientific research institutions' in order to develop alternatives (Jethani 2015). The individualised character of 'quantified self-experimentation' may take 'n=1' as its sample but is made meaningful only in relation to larger bodies of people and larger audiences with which data can be compared, and with institutions capable of articulating these links up to the level of whole populations.

CONCLUSION

Along with some other examples (Khovanskaya et al. 2013), the above represents the developing thinking of an emergent but still relatively small field of inquiry. The review suggests the need for further research and practical experimentation into uses of self-tracking technology and especially the collective use of such technology. The challenge is to understand the potential of self-quantification technology for collective resistance strategies and a shared understanding of productivity and well-being – specifically work's bodily and mental impacts – around which workers can better understand their work, potentially as a basis to organise and bargain. There is always a dual character to measurement in the workplace. It can be used by management to dominate workers but can also be used by those same workers to organise around and negotiate improvements in programmes of concerted collective bargaining. Shared forms of measurement present in the industrial workplace – such as the managerial clipboard of the Taylorist factory – saw established forms of measure used to both dominate workers and by those same workers to organise around and negotiate improvements in programmes of concerted collective bargaining. In this sense they represented a common, if contested, basis on which management and workforces could construct industrial compromises around time and productivity. But the fragmented and deregulated contemporary workplace often lacks clear frameworks of measure around which new compromises can be struck in pursuit of productivity gains and better working practices.

In light of this impasse, can distributed technologies of data capture and analysis through wearables and sensors support the remediation of industrial relations? Moreover, can the collective or aggregated quantification of the physical and emotional effects and impacts of working practices enable workers to better evidence, understand and negotiate around well-being issues, even in workplaces where the physical aspect of the work is not as transparent as in traditional industries? This could begin with subversion of existing top-down tracking or by developing entirely new measures for workers to collect data. This might incorporate, for instance, data that can be analysed algorithmically to identify and analyse certain patterns of movement (e.g. posture, or gait, speed/angle of getting up out of a chair). Charting the movement (of lack thereof) and expenditure of energy by workers in their places of work may help evidence the physical impacts of work even where these are not immediately apparent, in order to pursue improvements in workplace health and well-being. This data, in turn, could be combined with the collection and analysis of other kinds of individual and collective data around the practice and experience of work activities and the time in which they take place – e.g. wearable data and productivity management apps.

The question is how to collectivise what is currently a process of *individualised* and *individualising* commodification and control. What platforms, infrastructures and forms of ownership and permission are necessary to construct a framework for the shared 'bottom-up' collection and curation of individual data? The pooling and shared 'curation' of data may be one way to institutionalise a capacity for the data of quantification and self-quantification to be turned to the ends of a 'workers' inquiry' centring on 'sousveillance' as the bottom-up ability to monitor managerial practices against, and not in support of, exploitation and domination in the workplace. To realise this potential, we need to develop practical and empirical tools that will allow us to explore which kinds of data pooling might be useful and (importantly) acceptable to workers. As with any commons, it will also be necessary to determine how these self-tracking communities will be able to self-regulate so as to maximise the benefit for the community.

ACKNOWLEDGEMENTS

This research was funded by the ESRC Productivity Insights Network. Thanks to Freddie for research assistance, Donna Poade for her involvement at an earlier stage of the project, and Jamie Woodcock for comments on an earlier draft. Some elements of the chapter were developed in a blog for the Digital Societies Faculty Research Group at the University of Bristol.

REFERENCES

Cecchinato, M., Cox, A. L. and Bird, J. (2014). 'I Check My Emails on the Toilet': Email Practices and Work-Home Boundary Management. Conference: MobileHCI '14 Workshop: Socio-Technical Systems and Work-Home Boundaries.

Cecchinato, M., Cox, A. L. and Bird, J. (2015). Working 9–5? Professional Differences in Email and Boundary Management Practices. Proceedings of the 33rd Annual ACM Conference on Human Factors in Computing Systems.

Cecchinato, M., Cox, A. L. and Bird, J. (2017). Always On(line)? User Experience of Smartwatches and their Role within Multi-Device Ecologies. Conference: ACM 2017 CHI Conference on Human Factors in Computing Systems.

Daechong, H. A. (2017). Scripts and Re-scriptings of Self-Tracking Technologies: Health and Labor in an Age of Hyper-Connectivity. *Asia Pacific Journal of Health Law & Ethics* 10(3), 67–86.

Davies, W. (2019). The Political Economy of Pulse: Techno-Somatic Rhythm and Real-Time Data. *Ephemera* 19(3).

Elsden, C., Kirk, D. S. and Durrant, A. C. (2016). A Quantified Past: Toward Design for Remembering with Personal Informatics. *Human-Computer Interaction* 31(6), 518–57.

Eneman, M., Ljungberg, J., Rolsson, B. and Stenmark, D. (2018). Encountering Camera Surveillance and Accountability at Work: Case Study of the Swedish Police. UK Academy for Information Systems Conference Proceedings 2018.

Epstein, D., Cordeiro, F., Bales, E., Fogarty, J. and Munson, S. (2014). Taming Data Complexity in Lifelogs: Exploring Visual Cuts of Personal Informatics Data. Proceedings of the 2014 Conference on Designing Interactive Systems (DIS '14), 667–76.

Epstein, D., Ping, A., Fogarty, J. and Munson, S. (2015). A Lived Informatics Model of Personal Informatics. The 2015 ACM International Joint Conference on Pervasive and Ubiquitous Computing (UbiComp '15).

Freshwater, D., Fisher, P. and Walsh, E. (2013). Revisiting the Panopticon: Professional Regulation, Surveillance and Sousveillance. *Nursing Enquiry* 22(1).

Gardner, P. and Jenkins, B. (2015). Bodily Intra-actions with Biometric Devices. *Body & Society* 22(1).

Hänsel, K. (2016). Wearable and Ambient Sensing for Well-Being and Emotional Awareness in the Smart Workplace. Proceedings of the 2016 ACM International Joint Conference on Pervasive and Ubiquitous Computing (UbiComp '16).

Iqbal, S. T. et al. (2014). Bored Mondays and Focused Afternoons: The Rhythm of Attention and Online Activity in the Workplace. Proceedings of the SIGCHI Conference on Human Factors in Computing Systems (CHI '14), 3025–34.

Irani, L. C., and Silberman, M. S. (2013). Turkopticon: Interrupting Worker Invisibility in Amazon Mechanical Turk. Proceedings of the SIGCHI Conference on Human Factors in Computing Systems (CHI '13).

Jethani, S. (2015). Mediating the Body: Technology, Politics and Epistemologies of Self. *Communication, Politics & Culture* 14(3).

Kersten van-Dijk, E., Westerink, J. and Ijsselsteijn, W.A. (2016). Personal Informatics, Self-Insight, and Behavior Change: A Critical Review of Current Literature. *Human-Computer Interaction* 32(5–6), 268–96.

Khot, R., Horth, L. and Mueller, F. F. (2014). Understanding Physical Activity Through 3D Printed Material Artifacts. Proceedings of the SIGCHI Conference on Human Factors in Computing Systems (CHI '14), 3835–44.

Khovanskaya, V., Baumer, E. P., Cosley, D., Voida, S. and Gay, G. (2013). Everybody Knows What You're Doing: A Critical Design Approach to Personal Informatics. Proceedings of the SIGCHI Conference on Human Factors in Computing Systems (CHI '13), 3403–12.

Lascau, L., Gould, S. J. J., Cox, A. L., Karmannaya, E. and Brumby, D. P. (2019). Monotasking or Multitasking: Designing for Crowdworkers' Preferences. Proceedings of the 2019 CHI Conference on Human Factors in Computing Systems.

Li, I., Dey, A. and Forlizzi, J. (2010). A Stage-Based Model of Personal Informatics Systems. Proceedings of the SIGCHI Conference on Human Factors in Computing Systems, 557–66.

Lupton, D. (2014). Self-tracking Cultures: Towards a Sociology of Personal Informatics. Proceedings of the 26th Australian Computer-Human Interaction Conference (OzCHI '14), 77–86.

Maman, Z. S., Alamdar Yazdi, M. A., Cavuoto, L. A. and Megahed, F. M. (2017). A Data-Driven Approach to Modeling Physical Fatigue in the Workplace Using Wearable Sensors. *Applied Ergonomics* 65, 515–29.

Mann, S. (2002). Sousveillance, Not Just Surveillance, in Response to Terrorism. At http://n1nlf-1.eecg.toronto.edu/metalandflesh.htm.

Mathur, A., Van Den Broeck, M., Vanderhulst, G., Mashhadi, A. and Kawsar, F. (2015). Tiny Habits in the Giant Enterprise: Understanding the Dynamics of a Quantified Workplace. Proceedings of the ACM International Joint Conference on Pervasive and Ubiquitous Computing (UbiComp '15).

Moore, P. (2018a). *The Quantified Self in Precarity: Work, Technology and What Counts*. London and New York: Routledge.

Moore, P. (2018b). Tracking Affective Labour for Agility in the Quantified Workplace. *Body & Society* 24(3), 39–67.

Moore, P. (2019). E(a)ffective Precarity, Control and Resistance in the Digitalised Workplace. In D. Chandler and C. Fuchs, eds. *Digital Objects, Digital Subjects: Interdisciplinary Perspectives on Capitalism, Labour and Politics in the Age of Big Data*. London: University of Westminster Press, 125–44.

Moore, P. and Piwek, L. (2017). Regulating Wellbeing in the Brave New Quantified Workplace. *Employee Relations* 39(3), 308–16.

Moore, P. and Robinson, A. (2015). The Quantified Self: What Counts in the Neoliberal Workplace. *New Media & Society* 18(11), 2774–92.

Morgan, H. M. (2014). Research Note: Surveillance in Contemporary Health and Social Care: Friend or Foe?' *Surveillance & Society* 12(4), 594–6.

Neff, G. and Nafus, D. (2016). *Self-Tracking*. Cambridge, MA: MIT Press.

Pitts, F. H., Jean, E. and Clarke, Y. (2020). Sonifying the Quantified Self: Rhythmanalysis and Performance Research in and Against the Reduction of Life-Time to Labour-Time. *Capital & Class* 44(2), 219–40.

Rooksby, J. et al. (2014). Personal Tracking as Lived Informatics. Proceedings of the SIGCHI Conference on Human Factors in Computing Systems (CHI '14).

Schall, M. J., Sesek, R. F. and Cavuoto, L. A. (2018). Barriers to the Adoption of Wearable Sensors in the Workplace: A Survey of Occupational Safety and Health Professionals. *Human Factors: The Journal of the Human Factors and Ergonomics Society* 60(3), 351–62.

Whooley, M. et al. (2014). On the Integration of Self-Tracking Data Amongst Quantified Self Members. Proceedings of the 28th International BCS Human-Computer Interaction Conference (HCI '14), 151–60.

Wolf, G. (2019). Know Thyself: Tracking Every Facet of Life, from Sleep to Mood to Pain, 24/7/365. Wired. At www.wired.com/2009/06/lbnp-knowthyself.

Wood, A. J., Graham, M., Lehdonvirta, V. and Hjorth, I. (2019). Good Gig, Bad Gig: Autonomy and Algorithmic Control in the Global Gig Economy. *Work, Employment and Society* 33(1), 56–75.

11
Breaking Digital Atomisation: Resistant Cultures of Solidarity in Platform-Based Courier Work

Heiner Heiland and Simon Schaupp

The labour process on digital platforms, especially in the food-delivery sector, has been the subject of much research. Most studies agree that in this context a new regime of tight algorithmic control is emerging (Ivanova et al. 2018; Wood et al. 2019). Many of these studies emphasise the tendency of AI and algorithmic control to atomise workers and thus make collective resistance unlikely (e.g. Mahnkopf 2020; Veen, Barratt and Goods 2019). Shoshana Zuboff (2019) states that the ubiquity of digital sensor technology has finally eliminated all zones of uncertainty from the labour process by total surveillance. However, other studies claim that the opposite is the case: platform workers, especially in the food-delivery branch, are leading a new wave of strikes and direct actions in fighting for their labour rights (Cant 2019; Leonardi et al. 2019; Tassinari and Maccarrone 2019). Most of these struggles take place outside official union structures in grassroots unions or informal groups. Cant calls this the 'invisible organisation' (2019: 130–3). This chapter addresses the question of how these 'invisible organisations' are born. How is this unlikely occurrence of high-intensity workers' struggles possible if, at the same time, workers face atomisation and surveillance, which hinder solidarity and resistance? In answering this question, we emphasise the role of communicative cultures in fostering solidarity among workers.

Platform work in general is limited, with 0.5 per cent EU-wide (Eurofound 2017) and 0.9 per cent in Germany (Bonin and Rinne 2017) fulfilling the criteria of food delivery. In Germany, food-courier services (since 2014) have been among the most important forms of locally linked labour mediated via platforms. In 2019, the prospective turnover of food deliveries in general amounted to 1.8 billion euros, an increase of 14 per cent compared to 2018 (Statista 2019). Foodora and Deliveroo were the two central platforms during the study period – February–November 2018.[1] Approximately 5,000 riders, as the couriers are called – worked for the two platforms at that time. In the German case, at Deliveroo – as is usually the case in other countries – the riders are self-employed. At Foodora, however, the couriers are employed. As the figures show, the relevance of the phenomenon is not (yet) based on its size. Rather, this form of work is a techno-organisational avant-garde situation, and a test field for new forms of digital labour coordination and control which is characterised mainly by algorithmic work control. This aims at a technical 'autonomisation' of capital from labour and reaches far beyond the platform economy (Schaupp and Diab 2019). Algorithmic work control is, however, also a laboratory for solidarity and new forms of collective struggles (Schaupp 2018).

In order to investigate the phenomenon from a sociological perspective, two case studies of the two relevant platforms were carried out (Yin 2018). A 'fully integrated mixed design' was used (Teddlie and Tashakkori 2006), combining four elements: a quantitative online survey (Heiland 2019); semi-structured qualitative interviews (Kaufmann 2015); ethnography and content analysis of forums; and chat groups. A total of 47 interviews were carried out with food couriers from seven different German cities. The selection of the interviewees was based on theoretical sampling (Glaser and Strauss 1967). In addition, the authors themselves worked as couriers for Foodora and Deliveroo, conducting participant observations in six different cities over a period of eight months. In this way, it was possible to gain access to implicit process knowledge. Transcripts of the interviews, excerpts from forums and chats and field notes were coded and analysed using qualitative data analysis software (Kuckartz 2016).

In addition to these methods, a quantitative online survey was conducted. The aim of this survey was to gain explorative and descriptive insights into the phenomenon. Based on the qualitative findings, a targeted sampling strategy was pursued, and couriers were recruited for the survey to avoid self-selection biases (Barratt, Ferris and Lenton 2015). Thus, 251 partici-

1. At the end of 2018 Foodora was sold to its competitor Takeaway, and in August 2019 Deliveroo announced its withdrawal from Germany, thus consolidating the German market.

pants could be reached – approximately 5–10 per cent of the population (2,500–5,000 riders in Germany) at the time of the survey. In addition, a number of items were structured analogously to the DGB index 'Gute Arbeit' (Good Work), a representative survey of working conditions in Germany, so that results can be directly compared and contrasted to data driven from a representative sample of dependent employees in Germany.

Based on this data, the chapter argues that while the platforms aim for full control over the labour process and a radical atomisation of their riders, in practice the everyday reality is different. The riders manage to maintain a high level of inter-communication, using online tools and face-to-face meetings during working times. In his ground-breaking ethnographic study, Fantasia (1989) showed that cultures of solidarity are the basis for collective workers' struggles. We argue that such cultures are created by the different kinds of deviant communications that platform couriers manage to maintain. These cultures, in turn, enable various forms of self-organisation that seem unlikely in an atomised labour process.

CONTESTED COMMUNICATION

One of the central characteristics of platform work is the formal detachment of the workers from the companies. In the case of the food-delivery platforms, most riders never meet their supervisors in person. Instead, control is automated in the form of algorithmic management via the smartphone app that steers the labour process. The two central control strategies of the platform companies are digital tracking of the riders' movements, and the atomisation of the riders, which aims to prevent self-organisation and resistance (Cant 2019; Ivanova et al. 2018). Our data, however, demonstrate that the riders still find ways to outwit the digital surveillance and to establish a high level of communication amongst themselves. In the following, we will focus on the aspect of communication as a basis for the emergence of solidarity.

Contrary to the thesis of isolated platform workers, our online survey shows that the riders maintain a lively exchange with each other (see Figure 11.1): 60 per cent of the sample say they have contact with other riders often or very often, and 62 per cent say they have contact outside the actual work.

One important reason for the surprisingly high intensity of communication among the riders is the need for the exchange in order to be able to handle

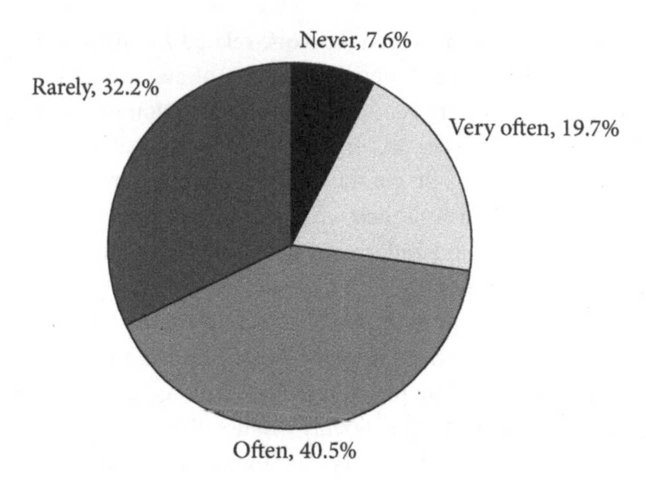

Figure 11.1 How Often Do You Interact With Other Drivers While Working?

the labour process. The functions of the app are constantly changed by the platform, which in turn alters the labour process: 'It is always changing ... They are testing all the time', as a rider describes the sometimes weekly app updates. Additionally, there is a high turnover of workers, since most of them stay only for several months and many only work a few hours every week. Therefore, even to keep normal operations running, some information exchange is necessary. In traditional companies, the transmission of this information would be the task of human resources departments. In the food platforms, however, it is delegated completely to the workers themselves. As a result, 70 per cent of respondents do not feel sufficiently informed by the company about decisions or changes that are affecting their work. As management is highly automated, most riders never meet their superiors. Neither can they reach them via telephone. Instead, riders must contact the dispatchers via the app in urgent instances during the labour process, and may contact the offices of the platforms via email for general and non-urgent questions. However, the latter have very long response times. A former manager says: 'Communication is extremely difficult. Nothing is being responded to. There is no response.' Both Foodora and Deliveroo therefore urge the riders to solve their problems themselves or ask their colleagues. To do so, the platforms established online chat groups for all the riders in one city (Foodora) or a centralised chat platform for all riders (Deliveroo).

These chat rooms are also used for work-related self-help. A wide variety of topics are discussed, including expressions of anger about nuisances at work. This reflects the very low level of job satisfaction of the riders: on an eleven-level scale from 'very dissatisfied' to 'very satisfied', the average value of the interviewees is 5.74. In contrast, other employees in Germany are significantly more satisfied with their work, according to the DGB index, with an average value of 7.49. Similarly, 60 per cent of the riders in the sample state that they do not identify with their job at all or only to a small extent – compared to 13 per cent in the DGB index. As a result, only just under 14 per cent of those surveyed say they see no reason for a strike or protest in their current work situation, meaning 86 per cent do.

Many of these problems were openly discussed in the chat forums. As an activist rider explained in an interview: 'that was the organising wonderland'. Deliveroo reacted to open organising by censoring the chat. When the riders began discussing whether to found a works council,[2] the chat option was shut down completely. Subsequently, Deliveroo implemented an app-internal chat, which only enabled communication between platform and courier and not between the riders. A former manager describes the reasons for closing the chat as follows:

> a) because they have introduced the Rider Support Chat into the app and b) because the obvious assumption was that this would involve too much arguing and danger of intercommunication. Of course, this was not very smart, because intercommunication then simply took place without us knowing. And that was the basic intention behind opening the chat ourselves.

Accordingly, parallel autonomous chat groups had been formed earlier, so that the riders could easily switch over to them. In these groups, relevant work information is exchanged. At the same time, a culture of solidarity is observable. The riders swap shifts, warn each other about restaurants with long waiting times, support each other in case of bicycle damage or by lending a bicycle or even offering places to sleep. In one case, after a rider

2. Works councils are institutions specific to the German model of industrial relations. The German Works Constitution Act grants workers the right to elect a works council at the company level. It has specific rights to information and co-determination but is restricted by a 'peace obligation', i.e. it cannot call for strikes, etc. (Müller-Jentsch 1995).

was involved in an accident, there was a call for donations in a nationwide chat: 'We're organising a little fundraising campaign for him among riders. I suppose no one here is rich, but if we act together and everyone donates a little bit, it'll already do the work. Speeding idiots can hit anyone of us at any time. So let's show that we don't leave people behind.' Some riders also used the chat groups to create 'peer to peer groups to help each other with our tax declaration'. In addition, issues that do not directly involve the labour process, such as political or cultural topics, are also addressed in the groups. Criticism of the working conditions is also freely expressed and discussed in these chats. Furthermore, an across-platform group with over 600 members exists, in which riders from different cities or even countries exchange views, as well as chats with over 100 participants in which protest and the efforts of the works councils are discussed.

Thus, while the origin of these chat groups lies in the need to facilitate exchange on the labour process and its organisation, the communication reaches way beyond that. Both the official and in particular the unofficial chat groups offer the opportunity to overcome the isolation of platform work. The platform-dominated face-to-interface communication contrasts with the chat group as a self-organised alternative. Although the shared workplace is the entire city, there are opportunities for virtual exchange that produce communitisation while also enabling analogue interactions.

However, face-to-face interactions play a central role for the couriers. These are not unusual at the beginning of a shift. In this respect, the platforms have decided against control of the workers and their atomisation and for the efficiency of the delivery process: shifts can only be started within a narrow radius around the clearly defined centre of the delivery zone. If the riders do not get a new order immediately after completing a job, they are encouraged to move to the centre of the zone, because most of the restaurants are located in the surroundings of the centres and thus the likelihood of receiving further orders is increased. When the riders see new colleagues in the street, they usually tell them where the couriers meet during the breaks. The intended atomisation of the riders through the platforms is thereby avoided:

> After the first two hours I met the other riders working in this zone several times in the street or in the usual restaurants. As the midday peak of orders fades, we all meet at the [zone centre] and have a few minutes

to chat. One of the riders asks us which chat groups we are in and if we are interested in discussing the working conditions via chat and if there is anything we can do.

Thus, the zone centre fulfils a crystallising function for the emergence of cultures of solidarity.

SELF-ORGANISATION

As we will show in the following, with the attempt to initiate organised resistance in the form of strikes and protests, and to institutionalise labour relations by means of the election of works councils, communication among the riders becomes first and foremost a concrete object of conflict. Despite the adverse organisational conditions, the young field of platform-mediated food-courier work is particularly prone to conflict.

Initial attempts by the riders to gain support from the traditional trade unions NGG and ver.di failed.[3] The respective unions had identified the field as 'unorganisable' due to high fluctuation and low salaries. Platform workers in other countries had had similar experiences before (Woodcock and Graham 2020: 109–11). However, this did not lead to a slackening of the workers' willingness to fight. On the contrary, they now turned to more radical grassroots unions (Cant 2019; Leonardi et al. 2019; Tassinari and Maccarrone 2019). In Germany, this was the anarcho-syndicalist Freie Arbeiter Union (FAU). In January 2018, for example, the riders organised in the FAU and demonstrated for a fair refund for wear and tear by collectively unloading their bicycle scrap in front of the headquarters of Delivery Hero, Foodora's parent company (Deliverunion 2018). Previously, the riders had forced Delivery Hero to the negotiation table with various bicycle demonstrations and logout actions. Their main demands were an increase in hourly wages by at least one euro, coverage of all repair costs by the company, and improvements in the shift planning system. When negotiations failed, the riders protested in front of a Foodora office in Berlin Mitte and occupied it temporarily. After the protests of the Berlin riders, a flat rate for wear and tear was introduced. However, it is not paid out, but accumulated as credit

3. NGG is the official trade union for the food sector; ver.di is the united services union. Both are organized in the German Trade Union Confederation (DGB), in which every trade union has its own uncontested domain.

in a web shop, which is considerably more expensive than a normal bicycle shop. In addition, the credit expires at regular intervals.

At the same time, another type of riders' movement arose, first in Cologne and then in Hamburg. This aimed at the election of works councils and – at least in the case of Foodora – successfully established them. There were later efforts to establish works councils at Foodora branches in many other cities as well. The protest landscape in Germany is thus divided. While in Berlin the riders try to improve the working conditions with the help of the FAU by means of direct action, at most of the other locations they try to install works councils – with the support of the NGG, which, after its initial scepticism and the first protest successes of the riders, took up the field and raised it to a pilot project. By the end of 2019, works councils existed at Foodora in five cities and one region, supplemented by a joint council concerning the whole platform.

Based on their various communication channels, riders in Cologne were the first to be able to elect a works council, despite many obstacles. At Foodora in Cologne, the council was elected in July 2017, and at Deliveroo in February 2018. At that time a large number of riders were still salaried rather than self-employed at Deliveroo in Cologne. The works council elections were prepared undercover in autonomous chat groups, which could only be joined by invitation. One activist remembers: 'The riders all had temporary contracts and some of them were still in the probationary period ... At first, things only proceeded cautiously.'

After the successful election of the works council, Deliveroo changed its business model. The contracts of the employed riders were allowed to expire and from then on the platform worked only with self-employed riders throughout Germany. As a result, the members of the works council lost their employment and the committee existed for only three months. Deliveroo thus embarked on the path to a 'post corporate society' (Davis 2017).

At Foodora, the organising for the works council election was primarily carried out via face-to-face communication at the starting point of the shifts. There, activists addressed other riders, who could only begin their shift within the narrow radius of this square. Since the successful election, the works council has been influencing the working conditions to the best of its ability. Cologne, for example, was the only location in Germany where the establishment of performance-based shift allocation was prevented. In contrast to Deliveroo, Foodora thus reluctantly, and in individual cities, adopted the German model of industrial relations (Silvia 2013). The successful election of works councils is proof of the riders' ability to organise, notwithstanding their comprehensive heteronomy and reputation for being 'unorganisable'. Nevertheless, as we have shown, such institutionalised solidarity does not emerge from nowhere. Its central foundations are the communication among the riders that exists despite the intended isolation and the resulting cultures of solidarity, which persist in open conflict with the platforms and expand the possibilities of action for the riders.

CONCLUSIONS

Cultures of solidarity are the basis for collective workers' struggles (Fantasia 1989). Solidarity, however, does not directly emerge out of shared objective interests, but also relies on everyday communication (Zoll 1988). We have demonstrated that delivery platform companies aim at atomising their workers by means of AI – or, more specifically, algorithmic work control – and thus they are preventing workers' self-organisation. However, our survey shows that 60 per cent of the riders in Germany are in contact with their colleagues often or very often. This is enabled by official and (more often) unofficial chat groups as well as by informal face-to-face meetings during work. Criticism of the working conditions is one of the major themes of this communication, which reflects the very low level of job satisfaction among the riders. Many of the online and face-to-face communication networks are thus used to organise for collective struggles that aim to improve working conditions. Initially, this self-organisation remained largely outside official trade union structures, as more radical grassroots unions became central in mobilising riders all over Europe. Once this had achieved initial successes in bargaining and gaining media attention, official trade unions stepped in and helped to begin to install works councils.

Taken together, the formal and informal struggles for platform workers' rights demonstrate the high potential for conflict around AI and algorithmic work control (Schaupp 2018). Ultimately, these findings demonstrate the failure of management's attempt to use AI to undermine collective organising. They therefore challenge techno-deterministic accounts that see a complete atomisation of workers as the consequence of the introduction of AI into the labour process.

REFERENCES

Barratt, M. J., Ferris, J. A. and Lenton, S. (2015). Hidden Populations, Online Purposive Sampling, and External Validity. *Field Methods* 27(1), 3–21.

Bonin, H. and Rinne, U. (2017). *Omnibusbefragung zur Verbesserung der Datenlage neuer Beschäftigungsformen*. IZA Research Report No. 80.

Braverman, H. (1998). *Labor and Monopoly Capital.* New York: Monthly Review Press.

Brinkmann, U. and Heiland, H. (2020). Liefern am Limit. Wie die Plattformökonomie die Arbeitsbeziehungen verändert. *Industrielle Beziehungen* 27(1): 120–40.

Brinkmann, U. and Seifert, M. (2001). 'Face to Interface': Zum Problem der Vertrauenskonstitution im Internet am Beispiel von elektronischen Auktionen. *Zeitschrift für Soziologie* 30(1), 23–47.

Cant, C. (2019). *Riding for Deliveroo: Resistance in the New Economy.* Cambridge: Polity.

Davis, G. F. (2017) Organization Theory and the Dilemmas of a Post-Corporate Economy. In J. Gehman, M. Lounsbury and R. Greenwood, eds. *How Institutions Matter!* Bingley: Emerald, 311–32.

Deliverunion (2018). Riders Unite! Protest at the Offices of Foodora. FAU. At https://deliverunion.fau.org/2018/01/17/riders-unite-protest-at-the-offices-of-foodora.

Eurofound (2017). *Non-Standard Forms of Employment: Recent Trends and Future Prospects.* At www.eurofound.europa.eu/publications/customised-report/2017/non-standard-forms-of-employment-recent-trends-and-future-prospects.

Fantasia, R. (1989). *Cultures of Solidarity: Consciousness, Action and Contemporary American Workers.* Berkeley: University of California Press.

Glaser, B. G. and Strauss, A. L. (1967). *Grounded Theory. Strategies for Qualitative Research.* Chicago: Aldine.

Heiland, H. (2018). Algorithmus = Logik + Kontrolle. Algorithmisches Management und die Kontrolle der einfachen Arbeit. In D. Houben and B. Prietl, eds. *Datengesellschaft. Einsichten in die Datafizierung des Sozialen.* Bielefeld: transcript, 233–52.

Heiland, H. (2019). Plattformarbeit im Fokus. Ergebnisse einer explorativen Online-Umfrage. *WSI Mitteilungen* 72(4), 298–304.

Ivanova, M., Bronowicka, J., Kocher, E. and Degner, A. (2018). *The App as a Boss? Control and Autonomy in Application-Based Management* (Arbeit | Grenze | Fluss – Work in Progress interdisziplinärer Arbeitsforschung Nr. 2). Frankfurt (Oder): Viadrina.

Kaufmann, J. C. (2015). *Das verstehende Interview.* Konstanz/Munich: UVK.

Kuckartz, U. (2016). *Qualitative Inhaltsanalyse. Methoden, Praxis, Computerunterstützung.* Weinheim: Beltz Juventa.

Leonardi, D., Murgia, A., Briziarelli, M. and Armano, E. (2019). The Ambivalence of Logistical Connectivity: A Co-Research with Foodora Riders. *Work Organisation, Labour & Globalisation* 13, 155–71.

Mahnkopf, B. (2020). The Future of Work in the Era of 'Digital Capitalism'. *Socialist Register* 56.
Müller-Jentsch, W. (1995) Germany: From Collective Voice to Co-management. In J. Rogers and W. Streeck, eds. *Works Councils: Consultation, Representation, and Cooperation in Industrial Relations*. Chicago: University of Chicago Press, 53–78.
Schaupp, S. (2018) From the 'Führer' to the 'Sextoy': The Techno-Politics of Algorithmic Work Control. At https://medium.com/sci-five-university-of-basel/from-the-f%C3%BChrer-to-the-sextoy-af6b68c634fc.
Schaupp, S. and Diab, R. S. (2019) From the Smart Factory to the Self-Organisation of Capital: 'Industrie 4.0' as the Cybernetisation of Production. *Ephemera*. At http://ephemerajournal.org/contribution/smart-factory-self-organisation-capital-%E2%80%98industrie-40%E2%80%99-cybernetisation-production.
Statista (2019). *Digital Market Outlook*. At www.statista.com/outlook/374/137/online-food-delivery/germany?currency=eur#market-revenue.
Silvia, S. J. (2013). *Holding the Shop Together: German Industrial Relations in the Postwar Era*. Ithaca: Cornell University Press.
Tassinari, A. and Maccarrone, V. (2019). Riders on the Storm: Workplace Solidarity among Gig Economy Couriers in Italy and the UK. *Work, Employment and Society* 34(1), 35–54.
Teddlie, C. and Tashakkori, A. (2006). A General Typology of Research Designs Featuring Mixed Methods. *Research in the Schools* 13(1), 12–28.
Veen, A., Barratt, T. and Goods, C. (2019). Platform-Capital's 'App-etite' for Control: A Labour Process Analysis of Food-Delivery Work in Australia. *Work, Employment and Society* 34(3), 388–406.
Wood, A. J., Graham, M., Lehdonvirta, V. and Hjorth, I. (2019). Good Gig, Bad Gig: Autonomy and Algorithmic Control in the Global Gig Economy. *Work, Employment and Society* 33(1), 56–75.
Woodcock, J. and Graham, M. (2020). *The Gig Economy: A Critical Introduction*. Cambridge: Polity.
Yin, R. K. (2018). *Case Study Research and Applications: Design and Methods*. London: Sage.
Zoll, R. (1988). Von der Arbeitersolidarität zur Alltagssolidarität. *Gewerkschaftliche Monatshefte* 6, 368–81.
Zuboff, S. (2019). *The Age of Surveillance Capitalism: The Fight for the Future at the New Frontier of Power*. Profile Books: London.

12

Resisting the Algorithmic Boss: Guessing, Gaming, Reframing and Contesting Rules in App-Based Management

Joanna Bronowicka and Mirela Ivanova

Don't believe the hype – the new fee system is a trap! Come together now!

Invitation to Deliverunion meeting in Berlin[1]

In December 2018 a group of over 30 food-delivery couriers, activists and researchers gathered in Berlin to discuss the new payment system implemented by Deliveroo. Instead of paying the same fee for each delivery, the company would price each order differently based on the distance between the restaurant and the customer. The new algorithmic rule used was not revealed to the workers, so the riders active in the FAU union organised a meeting to share the information they had gathered thus far. First, riders from France and the UK explained over Skype how the new scheme deteriorated their working conditions. Then, a rider presented how he had 'reverse engineered' the algorithm to approximate the formula used to calculate the new pay rate.

As riders speculated about the algorithm, we asked ourselves – should this type of guessing count as collective resistance? What conditions made this form of resistance necessary and possible? Drawing on our own case study of Deliveroo and Foodora riders in Berlin, we decided to look beyond the public collective actions such as protests or strikes, and focus on the hidden practices of resistance to the algorithmic management. Between March 2018 and January 2019, we conducted semi-structured interviews with 20

1. Deliverunion was a joint initiative of Foodora and Deliveroo riders supported by the FAU union in Berlin. See https://deliverunion.fau.org/2018/11/27/dont-believe-the-hype-the-new-fee-system-is-a-trap-come-together-now/#more-432.

riders and six company representatives. Although the two companies used different employment models – Deliveroo riders in Berlin were self-employed while Foodora riders were employees – their digital strategies to control workers' autonomy were strikingly similar.

We also carried out observations of rider interactions at work, after hours and during union meetings. We attempted to capture the conditions of opposition to the algorithmic management, the reasons behind it and the moments at which it was most likely to occur. We selected participants using the 'chain referral sampling method' and tried to ensure that respondents 'reflect what are thought to be the general characteristics of the population in question' (Biernacki and Waldorf 1981: 155). Our sample was quite heterogeneous: it contained both union members and riders who are critical towards unions, passionate bikers and those who dislike riding, part-time and full-time workers, migrants and German nationals, men and women.

We found that being subject to algorithmic management adds a 'digital' layer to an already precarious condition – in other words, the sense of insecurity is only deepened by digital characteristics such as an information vacuum, the lack of a feedback mechanism and data-driven performance control. We discovered that many collective practices in response to app-based management concern guessing the algorithmic rules, and bypassing them, but also reframing them in such a way that they can be contested. We conclude that practices hidden from the public eye could be considered resistance when they expose and challenge the power imbalance between the workers and the platforms.

ALGORITHMIC MANAGEMENT AND RESISTANCE

Practices of contestation need to be analytically located within the 'terrain' of a specific management regime (Edwards 1979), as different models generate 'their own contradictions and conditions' for resistance (Ackroyd and Thompson 2016: 188). The model of digital labour platforms aims to save labour costs by relying on a workforce made up of independent contractors or, rarely, short-term employees (Srnicek 2017), while high turnover and poor bargaining power (Vandaele 2018) add to the precarious working conditions. The particularity of the management regime of platforms relies on the technical ability to control the labour process of their workers through 'a distinctive, digital-based "point of production"' (Gandini 2019: 1044) – in this case the mobile app which embodies 'the rules of the game', continuously updated in 'a constant process of innovation and experimentation' (Ivanova et al. 2018: 10).

At first glance, app-based work does not seem to be a fertile ground for oppositional practices. Payment per gig, data-driven control, high turnover and physical isolation prevent the emergence of shared experiences, understandings and norms (Graham and Woodcock 2018). However, researchers have documented a wide variety of resistance practices in algorithmic workplaces, from protests and strikes, to efforts to build work councils, providing evidence that insurrection against the power of platforms is indeed feasible (Animento, Di Cesare and Sica 2017; Ecker, Le Bon and Emrich 2018; Degner and Kocher 2018; Chen 2018; Vandeale 2018; Herr 2017). Moreover, a survey of recent studies on crowd- and gig-workplaces reveals the importance of creating spaces for in-group expression outside of the platform boundaries, such as online forums or social media (Yin et al. 2016; Rosenbalt and Stark 2016; Wood et al. 2019). In contrast to public resistance practices, such as protests or strikes, the nature of individual and collective hidden practices is more ambiguous and sometimes dismissed as politically insignificant (Contu 2008). Yet, Mumby et al. propose that both public and hidden practices, called 'infrapolitics', can indeed be considered resistance when the 'prevailing structures of power are made visible, denaturalized, and the metrics for their operation is placed under scrutiny and questioned' (2017: 1164).

In the context of digital platforms, 'collective infrapolitics' can reveal information and power asymmetries between the platforms and the workers – for example by 'guessing' the opaque algorithms that translate workers' performance into data used to monitor and evaluate them (Möhlmann and Zalmanson 2017). In order to avoid the disciplinary grip of algorithmic management, Lyft and Uber drivers shared their mistakes and discoveries with others, pooled their observations and generated hypotheses about the rules of fare pricing or distribution (Allen-Robertson 2017). Through this collective process, workers construct theories, stories and urban legends (Möhlmann and Zalmanson 2017): the 'algorithmic imaginary' (Chan and Humphreys 2018) or the 'allegorithm' (Anderson 2016). Collective practices can then turn to 'gaming' the system or bypassing the rules of algorithmic management – Uber drivers deactivate the GPS to avoid punishment for rejecting unprofitable rides (Chan and Humphreys 2018), while

Didi drivers use different bot apps to catch the highest fares (Chen 2018). As the workers develop an understanding that the game is rigged over time, the 'allegorithm' fades and imaginaries can be deconstructed. A moral sense that algorithmic management is overly opaque and unfair makes workers suspicious (Shapiro 2018; Möhlmann and Zalmanson 2017). In reaction to this disenchantment, some of them might choose 'voice' as a strategy by constructing new frames and stirring change from within (Hirschman 1970).

Digital aspects of algorithmic management cannot easily be separated from other important circumstances such as payment per gig, high staff turnover or absence of union structures. In our findings, we turned our focus to these conditions and practices of resistance, which do appear unique to app-based management or, more broadly, digitally mediated labour.

FINDINGS

Interviews with the Foodora and Deliveroo riders revealed three 'digital' elements, which add to the already precarious working conditions – an information vacuum, the lack of feedback mechanisms, and the data-driven performance control.

The first condition of the 'digital precariat' is the shared experience of working in an information vacuum and in communicative isolation from other workers. Riders described 'being left alone with your questions' as a permanent condition perpetuated by frequent changes of the rules or the software design 'happening in an almost weekly rhythm, which makes you feel like a guinea pig'. They reported feeling 'confused', 'paranoid', 'afraid of getting fired … because you don't really get to understand all of the statistics', and compelled to learn the rules behind the algorithm, because 'it is so omnipresent; you need to deal with it all the time'. Yet, their attempts were frustrated by the lack of designated physical or digital spaces for worker interaction, described as deliberate attempts 'to prevent us from talking to each other'.

Riders were also isolated from company representatives and managers. Attempts to reach superiors by email were frustrating: 'it can take two or three working days to get a reply, but then you get a reply and you're never satisfied because they don't explain it enough'. One rider described the experience of being a voiceless worker by comparing emailing the office to 'shouting in the forest and hoping somebody is hearing'. Lack of voice or representation structures for workers prompted them to look for an alternative means of collectively addressing their needs.

Lastly, the experience of being subjected to data-driven performance evaluations also exacerbated the shared feeling of insecurity. Only the riders with the best statistics were given access to good shifts, while the others were left to compete for the remaining ones (Ivanova et al. 2018). For the riders with poorer statistics, access to profitable time slots and city zones was limited, leaving them feeling 'more insecure than ever'. The way the statistics were compiled was also deemed 'unfair' and 'ruthless', since it did not take into account reasons for being late or absent such as illness, accident, a broken bike or no internet access.

These shared conditions of app-based management gave rise to a collective experience of 'digital precarity': confusion, isolation, insecurity and lack of voice. They also fuelled the need to create new digital spaces for collective experiences and processes outside of the organisational boundaries. These self-organised communicative structures on WhatsApp, Slack or Facebook provided diverse opportunities for in-group identification, and generated new collective strategies to share information, to help each other, to express one's voice and, ultimately, to change the power relations at work.

GUESSING THE ALGORITHM: COLLECTIVE RULE-DISCOVERY PRACTICES

We found that Deliveroo and Foodora riders filled the information vacuum created by the app-based management by engaging in collective rule discovery. They collected information on their own, and shared it with others, thus translating individual hypotheses into collective theories. These collective practices of guessing the rules of the game often had the aim of regaining control over the working process, and challenging the legitimacy of the management regime.

Much of the communication in person or digitally was dedicated to 'guessing and gossiping' about the unknown rules of the app-based management. As a rider explained, 'of course, we all always speak about these things we don't know with my colleagues'. Our observations and interviews revealed that riders regularly tried to guess how the algorithm assigning orders works. They questioned if it is really only the GPS location and the proximity to the restaurant that is taken into account, or if other perimeters are playing a role too. Deliveroo riders were similarly perplexed about how the metrics of the shift sorting system works. While they knew that being late and missing a shift were the two criteria determining their position in the badge system, it was unclear how many times they should arrive on time in order to improve their standing. The practices of sharing experiential knowledge seemed especially valuable when one had just started the job. For example, riders reassured a new colleague that the notification 'Your acceptance rate is pending' was nothing to worry about: 'I have been refusing 4 or 5 [orders] in a row and it was OK.'

Practices of collective learning intensified when app changes were introduced, because riders were often not warned about new rules and were left to discover them alone. For example, when the platforms introduced a feature that would reveal the rider's name to the customer, the news was shared by word of mouth. Major design overhauls prompted the riders to share the results of their trial and error experiments with others, and discover how the app-based management actually works. When Foodora introduced a new shift-booking system, for instance, a rider learned that 'you only find out by playing basically. You need to game around or ask the people to game around.'

We discovered that the guessing contributed to the construction of a collective imaginary about the algorithmic rule. For example, when it came to the algorithm allocating orders, some riders believed that it was fair and equalised the number of orders per shift among the riders, while others believed that 'the faster you are, the longer distance orders you will get'. These imaginaries had behavioural consequences – some riders cycled slower to avoid being assigned long-distance gigs or rode the streets around the restaurant in the hope of getting the next order sooner.

The intention to share useful information rather than 'free-ride' on the information collected by others points to the political nature of this practice (Olson 1965; Jasper 2011). As some authors suggest, rule discovery and guessing the system 'often describe malicious attempts by a platform uninterested in drivers' wellbeing and success and encourage drivers' action and resistance' (Möhlmann and Zalmanson 2017: 11). Indeed, bringing clarity to a deliberately obscure rule design can be considered resistance – not if it's done for personal gain, but certainly when the goal is to expose unfair rules in a way that means they can be bypassed or challenged, and the balance of power tipped in favour of the workers.

GAMING THE SYSTEM: BYPASSING THE ALGORITHMIC RULES

Collective strategies practised by Deliveroo and Foodora riders went beyond learning the rules – their goal was to 'game' them and avoid punishment by the platform. For example, riders downloaded apps to spoof their GPS location, to cover up being late for a shift, and to protect their statistics. Also, they avoided the penalty for missing a shift by staying at home and rejecting all incoming orders. Rather than keeping these strategies private, riders eagerly shared information on how to 'game the system' by exploiting app design flaws and opportunities for misbehaviour. Without a physical boss, these practices were easier, because, as one rider observed, 'The app doesn't see everything ... so you can [pretend] that you are behaving like the company expects you to behave, but in fact, you are not.'

Our research suggests that the line between individual and collective gaming strategies is blurry, since individual misbehaviour can contribute to collective solidarity. When Deliveroo introduced a shift-booking system automatically sorting riders according to their statistics, the riders reacted by creating a 'black-market for shifts'. In defiance of the competition logic established by the company, riders with better statistics found a way to reassign profitable shifts to those with worse statistics – for no apparent personal gain. The political intent of this practice was clear – it exposed how the data-driven ranking system is unfair, because it can cause riders with lower statistics to lose their jobs. This shift-exchange practice is an example of the 'digital misbehaviour' or 'algorithmic activism' (Chen 2018) of platform workers who exploit the vulnerabilities of an app-based management system. It also shows that the shared experience of precarity in the gig economy can lead to the creation of informal networks of support and foster collective opposition.

We conclude that the shift-exchange practice, although invisible to the company and bystanders, should count as resistance, because it exposes the logic of control through competition and replaces it with the logic of solidarity. More broadly, we suggest that gaming strategies can be considered a form of resistance to algorithmic rules when they spark the collective questioning of their social design.

REFRAMING THE JOB: HIDDEN EXPRESSIONS OF DISSENT

We discovered that the same communicative structures used for sharing information about working rules could be quickly repurposed as spaces for collective expressions of grievances with the management. As riders reported, 'this was always a topic – the conditions and how Deliveroo is not doing good to the employees'. We observed that even when riders met to relax after work, the conversation quickly turned to sharing frustrations about the working conditions. The interviews also revealed grievances about the app-based management, in particular mistakes in the data collection and the lack of clarity about how statistics are used for automated sorting. Perplexed with his average speed of 38 km/hour, one rider wondered: 'The algorithm has calculated something but apparently there must be kind of a mistake ... you know, sometimes they just have wrong interpretations of the data or it leads to kind of wrong results.'

We also observed that when a company introduced sudden and unilateral changes to the management regime, the expressions of dissent intensified into a collective 'moral shock' (Jasper 2011). This is how a rider described a reaction on a WhatsApp group on the day the new shift system was introduced: 'There was a chat of, I think, a thousand lines. Everybody was going like *What the fuck are you doing? You fucking idiots!* ... It was a serious "fuck you" moment.' These moral shocks played an important role in worker mobilisation for collective action because they made it apparent that the management practices do not align with their own moral framework.

The subsequent reframing of the app-based management regime by the workers took place in spaces outside of the organisational boundaries and away from the supervisors' gaze. The app-based management regimes appear to have different affective politics than traditional workplaces, where management can simulate and standardise expressions of affect which 'prevents workers from establishing more traditional friendship and community networks' (Gregg 2010: 253). The workspace of Deliveroo and Foodora riders seemed free of such affective norms, which they considered an advantage of this type of work: 'here you don't have to smile and make everything look nice'. We suppose that absence of affective control can open a new space for 'affective solidarity' (Moore 2019), as well as collective expressions of dissent.

CONTESTING THE ALGORITHM: COLLECTIVE EXPRESSIONS OF VOICE

In addition to the hidden and ambiguous practices of guessing, gaming and reframing the working rules, we also observed that workers expressed their 'voice' publicly – either directly with the company management or through a union. The first strategy involved sharing grievances by sending management representatives emails, letters and messages on Slack, or addressing them directly in meetings. For example, when Deliveroo changed the criteria for receiving a bonus, a group of riders wrote a letter stating: 'This is definitely not correct and you can't just take away something that we are relying on so much.' Deliveroo riders requested a meeting to propose an alternative shift-booking system, which would allow for exchanging shifts between the riders. They also invited the company to join the Slack platform not only to be able to share their feedback with the company, but also to increase their visibility – or, as one rider put it, to let them know that 'we are here'. The followers of this first strategy believed that individual or collective expressions of voice had a positive impact on management decisions.

In contrast, the members of the Deliverunion campaign unionised in the FAU assumed that management is not likely to implement desirable changes unless pressured by the workers or the general public. The Deliveroo and Foodora riders who joined the campaign have succeeded in raising public awareness about the working conditions in food-delivery platforms through petitions, demonstrations and protests. In January 2018, Foodora riders protested by 'delivering' broken bike parts in front of the Berlin office of the parent company, Delivery Hero. In April 2018, Deliveroo riders 'delivered' a pizza box containing the signatures of 150 riders demanding better working conditions to the Berlin office. In addition to these actions reported by the media, the Deliveroo riders also organised a 'log-off strike' in one of the city zones, but fell short of the full rider participation needed to achieve a political impact.

The unexpected changes to digital conditions presented union organisers with opportunities for collective mobilisation. As a Foodora union member explained, the decision to reveal the rider name to the restaurant and the customer catalysed the Deliverunion campaign: 'that was actually the moment we started organising ourselves'. The union demands evolved with time, but at first they focused on working conditions – coverage of bike repair costs, higher wages and a guarantee of enough working hours per week. Later, the demands were more specific to the conditions of the app-based management – for example Deliveroo riders asked for better transparency about their working hours, and Foodora riders requested to be paid one hour per week for shift planning.

Actions such as protests, demonstrations or strikes were expressions of a collective voice not only towards the company, but also towards the general public and supporters of the worker movement. In the platform economy, the data-driven architecture causes workers to seem invisible, calculable and easily replaceable (van Doorn 2017), so publicly displaying their presence, discontent and opinions is undoubtedly a form of opposition. Ultimately, when workers fail 'to gain access to the flows of domination in order to participate in the decisions that affect them' by engaging with the management directly (Fleming and Spicer 2007: 48), public resistance is seen as the only and last resort.

DISCUSSION

The goal of our study was to understand the relationship between algorithmic management and the practices of resistance. We found that app workers engaged in a multitude of oppositional practices, despite obstacles typical to gig work, and specific to algorithmic workplaces. The practices of guessing, gaming, reframing and contesting the algorithmic rule were similar to what other scholars have described in other studies about app-based workplaces. Our results contribute to this line of inquiry by detailing the conditions of 'digital precarity' as well as the possibilities and forms of 'algorithmic resistance'.

First, we conclude that algorithmic management creates conditions of insecurity and instability resulting from the precarious employment model. These conditions include a communicative isolation and an information vacuum, a lack of voice and representation structures, and the use of data for controlling workers rather than supporting them. This type of management can certainly hinder organised resistance, but it can simultaneously foster shared experiences and needs that can only be addressed by collective practices of learning, solidarity and resistance. This resistance undermines the algorithmic rule. As Cant (2019) recognised, while precarity increases vulnerability it also sharpens class conflicts.

Second, we provide further examples of how workers can open new spaces for collective resistance by exploiting technological vulnerabilities. We develop the notion of 'algorithmic activism' by showing innovative ways to break or suspend the algorithmic rule (Chen 2018). From spoofing their GPS location in order to skip work without punishment, to exchanging profitable shifts between each other in the spirit of solidarity, workers can use their technical knowledge to distance themselves from the company's disciplinary logic. Gig workers are quick to add digital technologies to their struggles, as illustrated by the log-off strike which is an obvious response to the new model of work termed 'logged labor' (Huws 2016). The use of Slack shows that communication tools designed for other workplaces can be easily repurposed even in an environment without physical bosses. Each of these practices helps workers 'create some space and autonomy in order to exercise a degree of control' (Edwards, Collinson and Della Rocca 1995: 284), not only as individuals, but also as a group.

Finally, we conclude that hidden practices of algorithmic resistance can and should be counted as resistance when they have a political intent. Guessing and gaming are often more than merely 'coping strategies' without any intent to change the underlying power structures (Sauder and Espeland 2009; Chan and Humphreys 2018), but they constitute resistance when they put the algorithmic regime under scrutiny and question (Mumby et al. 2017). Indeed, the goal of collective rule discovery is to uncover the unfair metrics and rules, and gaming helps to tip the balance of power in favour of the worker. When done collectively, gaming strategies can lead to a reframing of the information asymmetry as unjust and put access to information at the centre of workers' demands.

In a well-designed game, players gradually discover the rules by trial and error. In the platform economy, however, workers are not meant to fully understand the game rules and experimentation is punished. These control mechanisms of the platform economy are in part a return to 'industrial systems' in the Western world (Cherry 2016), but twisted in a new way. As algorithmic management deepens the information asymmetries, traditional loci of struggle such as time, effort and wages merge with new disputes over access to information and algorithmic fairness. The way that workers, who are denied voice and representation by the platforms, practice novel forms of resistance can provide us with useful insights into the reconfigurations of power in the next era of industrial relations.

REFERENCES

Ackroyd, S. and Thompson, P. (2016). Unruly Subjects: Misbehaviour in the Workplace. In S. Edgell, H. Gottfried and E. Granter, eds. *The SAGE Handbook of the Sociology of Work and Employment*, London: SAGE, 185–204.

Allen-Robertson, J. (2017). The Uber Game: Exploring Algorithmic Management and Resistance. Paper at the 18th Annual Conference of the Association of Internet Researchers, Tartu, Estonia, 18–21 October. At https://core.ac.uk/download/pdf/132207403.pdf.

Anderson, D. N. (2016). Wheels in the Head: Ridesharing as Monitored Performance. *Surveillance & Society* 14(2), 240–58.

Animento S., Di Cesare, G. and Sica, C. (2017). Total Eclipse of Work? Neue Protestformen in der gig economy am Beispiel des Foodora Streiks in Turin. *PROKLA 187*, 47(2), 271–90.

Biernacki, P. and Waldorf, D. (1981). Snowball Sampling: Problems and Techniques of Chain Referral Sampling. *Sociological Methods & Research* 10(2), 141–63.

Cant, C. (2019). *Riding for Deliveroo: Resistance in the New Economy*. Cambridge: Polity.

Chan, N. K. and Humphreys, L. (2018). Mediatization of Social Space and the Case of Uber Drivers. *Media and Communication* 6(2), 29–38.

Chen, J. Y. (2018). Thrown Under the Bus and Outrunning It! The Logic of Didi and Taxi Drivers' Labour and Activism in the On-Demand Economy. *New Media & Society* 20(8), 2691–711.

Cherry, M. A. (2016). Beyond Misclassification: The Digital Transformation of Work. *Comparative Labor Law and Policy Journal* 37(3), 577–602.

Contu, A. (2008). Decaf Resistance. *Management Communication Quarterly* 21(3), 364–79.

Degner, A. and Kocher, E. (2018). Arbeitskämpfe in der 'Gig-Economy'? Die Protestbewegungen der Foodora- und Deliveroo-'Riders' und Rechtsfragen ihrer kollektiven Selbstorganisation. *Kritische Justiz* 51(3), 247–65.

Ecker, Y., Le Bon, M. and Emrich, S. (2018). Race Against the Machine: the Effects of Digitalization on the Working Conditions and the Organization of Labor Struggles. An Empirical Study on the Online Delivery Companies Deliveroo and Foodora in Berlin. *Projekt//raum working papers* #1.

Edwards, P., Collinson, D. and Della Rocca, G. (1995). Workplace Resistance in Western Europe: A Preliminary Overview and a Research Agenda. *European Journal of Industrial Relations* 1(3), 283–316.

Edwards, R. (1979). *Contested Terrain: The Transformation of Industry in the Twentieth Century*. London: Heinemann.

Fleming, P. and Spicer, A. (2007). *Contesting the Corporation: Struggle, Power and Resistance in Organizations*. Cambridge: Cambridge University Press.

Gandini, A. (2019). Labour Process Theory and the Gig Economy. *Human Relations* 72(6), 1039–56.

Graham, M. and Woodcock, J. (2018). Towards a Fairer Platform Economy: Introducing the Fairwork Foundation. *Alternate Routes* 29, 242–53.

Gregg, M. (2010). On Friday Night Drinks: Workplace Affects in the Age of the Cubicle. In M. Gregg and G. J. Seigworth, eds. *The Affect Theory Reader*. Durham, NC: Duke University Press, 250–68.

Herr, B. (2017). Riding in the Gig Economy: An In-Depth Study of a Branch in the App-Based on-Demand Food Delivery Industry. Working Paper No. 169, Chamber of Labour, Vienna. At www.arbeiterkammer.at/infopool/wien/AK_Working_Paper_Riding_in_the_Gig_Economy.pdf.

Hirschman, A. O. (1970). *Exit, Voice, and Loyalty: Responses to Decline in Firms, Organizations, and States*. Cambridge, MA: Harvard University Press.

Huws, U. (2016). Logged Labour: A New Paradigm of Work Organisation? *Work Organisation, Labour and Globalisation* 10(1), 7–26.

Ivanova, M., Bronowicka, J., Kocher, E. and Degner, A. (2018). The App as a Boss? Control and Autonomy in Application-Based Management. In *Arbeit | Grenze | Fluss – Work in Progress interdisziplinärer Arbeitsforschung 2*. Frankfurt (Oder): Europa-Universität Viadrina Frankfurt.

Jasper, J. M. (2011). Emotions and Social Movements: Twenty Years of Theory and Research. *Annual Review of Sociology* 37, 285–303.

Möhlmann, M. and Zalmanson, L. (2017). Hands on the Wheel: Navigating Algorithmic Management and Uber Drivers' Autonomy. Proceedings of the International Conference on Information Systems (ICIS 2017), 10–13 December, Seoul, South Korea.

Moore, P. (2019). E(a)ffective Precarity, Control and Resistance in the Digitalised Workplace. In D. Chandler and C. Fuchs, eds. *Digital Objects, Digital Subjects: Interdisciplinary Perspectives on Capitalism, Labour and Politics in the Age of Big Data*. London: University of Westminster, 125–44.

Mumby, D. K., Thomas, R., Martí, I. and Seidl, D. (2017). Resistance Redux. *Organization Studies* 38(9), 1157–83.

Nachtwey, O. and Staab, P. (2018). Das Produktionsmodell des digitalen Kapitalismus. *Soziale Welt*, Special issue, 23.

Olson, M. (1965). *The Logic of Collective Action: Public Goods and the Theory of Groups*. Cambridge, MA: Harvard University Press.

Rosenblat, A. and Stark, L. (2016). Algorithmic Labor and Information Asymmetries: A Case Study of Uber's Drivers. *International Journal of Communication* 10, 3758–84.

Sauder, M. and Espeland, W. N. (2009). The Discipline of Rankings: Tight Coupling and Organizational Change. *American Sociological Review* 74(1), 63–82.

Shapiro, A. (2018). Between Autonomy and Control: Strategies of Arbitrage in the 'On-Demand' Economy. *New Media & Society* 20(8), 2954–71.

Srnicek, N. (2017). *Platform Capitalism*. Cambridge: Polity.

van Doorn, N. (2017). Platform Labor: On the Gendered and Racialized Exploitation of Low-Income Service Work in the 'On-Demand' Economy. *Information, Communication & Society* 20(6), 898–914.
Vandaele, K. (2018). Will Trade Unions Survive in the Platform Economy? Emerging Patterns of Platform Workers' Collective Voice and Representation in Europe. ETUI Working Paper, 2018–05.
Wood, A. J., Graham, M., Lehdonvirta, V. and Hjorth, I. (2019). Good Gig, Bad Gig: Autonomy and Algorithmic Control in the Global Gig Economy. *Work, Employment and Society* 33(1), 56–75.
Yin, M., Gray, M. L., Suri, S. and Vaughan, J. W. (2016). The Communication Network Within the Crowd. Proceedings of the 25th International Conference on World Wide Web, 1293–303.

Notes on Contributors

Adam Badger is an interdisciplinary (Geography & Management) PhD student at Royal Holloway, University of London, investigating the lived experience of work in London's gig economy. His research utilises covert auto-ethnographic methods in order to investigate the phenomena in place, and as lived by workers, day to day.

Paško Bilić is a Research Associate at the Institute for Development and International Relations in Zagreb, Croatia. Previously, he was International Visiting Research Fellow at the Institute for Advanced Studies, University of Westminster, a short-term researcher at Istanbul Bilgi University and the University of Bremen, and a Doctoral Research Fellow at the University of Alberta, Canada.

Giorgio Boccardo is Assistant Professor in the Sociology Department at Universidad de Chile. He is co-author (with Carlos Ruiz) of *Chilenos bajo el neoliberalismo. Clases y Conflicto Social* (2014).

Joanna Bronowicka is a researcher at the Center for Interdisciplinary Labour Law Studies at the European University Viadrina in Frankfurt Oder. Previously, she was the director of the Centre for Internet and Human Rights.

Marta E. Cecchinato is a Senior Lecturer in the Computer and Information Science Department at Northumbria University. Her work focuses on understanding the complexities of dealing with technologies in everyday life and how digital experiences can be shaped to support well-being, at work and in personal life. Besides her publications in the field of Human-Computer Interaction, she has recently published a chapter in the *Oxford Handbook of Digital Technology and Society* (2020).

Beatriz Casas González is a researcher at the ISF München and a PhD candidate in the sociology of work at Hamburg University. Her PhD investigates how the technological and organisational changes introduced in German production companies affect workers' consciousness of domination.

Sandy J. J. Gould is a lecturer in Human-Computer Interaction in the School of Computer Science at the University of Birmingham. His research focuses on understanding relations between people, technology and work.

Heiner Heiland is assistant to the Chair of Sociology of Work and Organisations at the Technical University of Darmstadt. He is currently undertaking research on platform-mediated service work, temporary work and labour unions, and digitalisation, and has published on labour process control, workers' voice and digitalisation.

Benjamin Herr is a sociologist of work, interested in non-standard forms of employment, the gig economy and workplace organising.

Mirela Ivanova is a researcher and a PhD candidate in Sociology at the University of Basel. Previously, she was a researcher at the Centre for Internet and Human Rights and the Center for Interdisciplinary Labour Law Studies at the European University Viadrina in Frankfurt Oder.

Peter Kels trained as a sociologist and is Professor for Human Resource Management, Leadership and Innovation at Lucerne University of Applied Sciences & Arts. In his research, teaching and training activities, he focuses on the digital transformation of organisations, employee relations, changing careers and innovative human resource management and leadership practices.

Phoebe V. Moore works at the University of Leicester School of Business and is a Research Fellow at Weizenbaum Institute WZB in Berlin. Moore is a globally respected researcher on work and technology and an international leader and expert in this field, having given over 20 keynote lectures and published over 50 pieces on these topics, including three individually authored books. Her work impacts the International Labour Organization and the European Union via several commissioned high-level reports on work, technology and what counts.

Eduard Müller is a research associate and PhD candidate at the Institute of Sociology, Johannes Kepler University Linz. His major research interests lie in the sociology of work and employment as well as digital evaluative practices. His PhD thesis explores algorithmic bureaucracy within the Austrian public employment service.

Luca Perrig is a PhD candidate at the University of Geneva, Switzerland. His research interests currently focus on the technological intermediation taking place between managers and workers in the platform economy.

Frederick Harry Pitts is a lecturer in Work, Organisation and Public Policy at the University of Bristol School of Management, where he also leads the Faculty Research Group for Perspectives on Work. He is the author of *A World Beyond Work? Labour, Money and the Capitalist State Beyond Crisis and Utopia* (2021, with Ana Dinerstein) and *Value* (2020).

Toni Prug is an independent researcher based in Zagreb, Croatia. Previously, he was a teaching assistant and guest lecturer at the School of Business and Management, Queen Mary, University of London, where in 2014 he obtained his PhD on non-market and egalitarian production.

Simon Schaupp is assistant to the Chair for Social Structure Analysis at the University of Basel, Switzerland. He has published on the power effects of digital technologies and social self-organisation.

Uwe Vormbusch is Professor for the Analysis of Contemporary Societies at FernUniversität in Hagen. His areas of research are the sociology of quantification and valuation, economic and financial sociology, Artificial Intelligence and the moral fabric of life.

Jamie Woodcock is a senior lecturer at the Open University and a researcher based in London. He is the author of *The Gig Economy* (2019), *Marx at the Arcade* (2019) and *Working the Phones* (2017). His research is inspired by the workers' inquiry and focuses on labour, work, the gig economy, platforms, resistance, organising and videogames. He is on the editorial board of *Notes from Below* and *Historical Materialism*.

Index

AI refers to artificial intelligence; *fig* refers to a figure; *n* refers to a note